INDUS

D1023846

"Read it and then read i ....oellers gives a vast amount of con......................... to hopefuls trying to get in the door of this business without sugar coating the realities of it. Bravo!"

Marcie Robidart

Cosmopolitan/Osaka, Japan

"Finally! A comprehensive, no-holds-barred, no-nonsense inside look into the mysterious and unknown world of the modeling business. Marcia Rothschild compiles her years of experience and contacts to inform, educate and, above all, honestly provide insight into the business of professional modeling. From how to get started, to what agencies look for, to how to communicate with your agent, to spelling out dollars and cents, Marcia answers all questions for the potential model and his or her supporters. Kudos to you, Marcia, for this frank and easy to read guide!"

Lois Thigpen / Vice President, Agency Director

Elite Atlanta

"Not only does Marcia have an amazing talent for finding and developing models, but she has now proven her ability to completely capture the modeling ins and outs in this book. It is refreshing to know that finally there is a book to teach model hopefuls in a thorough and honest way. This is truly a great asset to any person researching or getting into the crazy world of modeling!"

Erin Lundgren, Director of Special Events

New York Model Management and LA Models

INDUSTRY PRAISE

"A must read for anyone contemplating entering the modeling world! Very comprehensive and insightful."

Joel Wilkenfeld / Co-President

Next Model Management Worldwide

"With the busy pace of this business, and large influx of models, I feel over the past 10 years, key, important elements for a beginning model have been lost. Marcia has recaptured these very important details in her book. She sheds some light for people who want to get into our industry."

James Charles / Director of New Faces

LA Models

"It is such a pleasure working with someone like Marcia in our industry. She is passionate about her work and she gives us her best from the heart. I can speak from experience and say Marcia has a vision for the modeling industry unlike anyone I know. She pursues our business with everything she has learned to-date. The advice she provides in her book has come from her years of experience in this industry as an agent, a manager, a model scout and a devoted mother to her three children. I know this upcoming book will serve as an informative and insightful tool for all that seek an honest angle into this business called "modeling." Thank you Marcia Rothschild Moellers."

Dan Hollinger / Director of New Faces

Kim Dawson Agency

INDUSTRY PRAISE

"Marcia has been in the business for a long time and has started many great careers. She has compiled information for this great book from her years of experience and many other agents. It is a must read if you want to succeed in the fashion world."

Susan Kaleta / Director

Page 214 Models / Dallas

"Love the book! Straight up! And in your face about the real world of this industry!"

Stacey Eastman / President

Pulse Management

"Hands down the best way to know what to expect when you don't know what to expect from the Modeling Industry! Thanks to Marcia for making things easier on agents as well as perspective models."

Ximena Peralta / Mens Division

Next Model Management

"Top to bottom, front to back this is the book every parent and their aspiring model should read. Marcia Rothschild Moellers is the Mother of the scouting / modeling industry; nobody knows the ins and outs of the modeling business better!"

David Grilli

Code Management

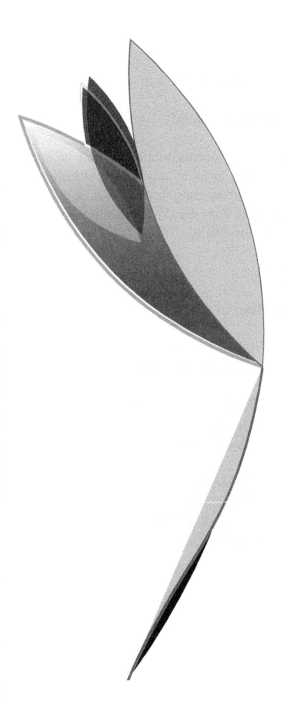

So, You Want To Be A Fashion Model?

by
Marcia
Rothschild Moellers

So, You Want to be a Fashion Model?
3rd printing
© 2005 Marcia Rothschild Moellers

ISBN: 0-9747920-0-4

Printed in the United States of America

Cover Design/ Typesetting:	Nurhan Thompson www.redperfect.com
Printed by:	Total Printing Systems Newton, IL www.tps1.com
Published by:	MRMoellers PO Box 3168 Estes Park, CO 80517 bravodbt@msn.com

PREFACE NOTE

I have been an agent for over twenty years. Unfortunately, due to a class action suit filed in New York City several years back, many of my colleagues are no longer allowed to call themselves "agents." I chose to leave New York City and to raise my family, and frankly, have a simpler life. I have watched my New York colleagues sacrifice their lives because of their passion for the fashion industry. In all businesses there are people that don't follow the appropriate professional standards, but I can truly say the majority of my peers are very, very ethical. In my opinion, my colleagues deserve far more money and credit than they will ever make. For that reason, I will refer to them in this book as "agents", which to me, they will always be and I see as an honor. God bless them all.

March 2005

DEDICATIONS

TO GOD AND ALL THE ANGELS.

Thank You for Your Unlimited Abundance With This Book and My Life. May this book serve you to share in all the creativity and abundance you offer.

TO MY LOVING FAMILY,

James, Jacob, Morgane & Madison. Thank you for everything you teach me. I love you so much.

TO MY SPIRITUAL TEACHERS AND FRIENDS,

Kia Portafekas, Mary Statum, Terry Johnson, Rosemary Barrie, Deborah Murphy, Marni Cobb, Hilliary Santos, Lenaye Hudock.

TO THE WONDERFUL NURHAN THOMPSON,

None of this would be possible without you. Thank you for being in the driver's seat.

TO THE AGENTS, AGENCIES AND CONVENTIONS,

For giving me the opportunity to meet and speak to thousands of young people, and all the help you have given me along the way.

TO MY FREINDS IN THE BUSINESS,

Who Have Helped Shape My Philosophies: Madeleine Aluri, Shoko Arai, Donna Baldwin (my "mother"), Brad Baldwin, Ivan Bart, Jan Berendsen, Robert Black, Greg Chan, James Charles, Mark Cook, JJ Cortez, Preston Davis, Robin Deal, Lynn DeLaney, Larry DiMarzio, Victoria Duruh, Anita Finkelstein, Diana Gormley, David Grilli, Justin Habel, Dan Hollinger, Greg James, Susanne Johnson, Darrin Judkins, Susan Kaleta, Karen Lee, Santiago Lopez-Guiz, Michel Lu, Erin Lundgren, Jack Maiden, Ingrid McAuliffe, Leah McCloskey, Anita Norris, Jovanna Papdakis, David Ralph, Marcie Robidart, Jane Stewart, Amy Tan, Lois Thigpen, Guido Toure, Roman Young & All the Agents, Who Work Selflessly, Love the Business, and Fight for Values & Integrity in our Industry.

TO ALL YOUNG HOPEFULS,

I hope this book inspires you to greatness and to always do your best in everything you do.

Table of Contents

Why **Write This Book** 11

1. Where **Do Hopefuls Start?** 13

2. The **Modeling Business**

   The Big Picture 17

3. Taking **Your Self-Assessment** 21

4. The **Outer You** 23

5. The **Inner You** 69

6. Your **Life** 89

7. Reality **Checks** 105

8. Final **Countdown**

   Snapshot Procedure 109

   Snapshot Examples 122

9. Pursuing **Representation** 127

10. The **Ultimate "Yes"** 147

11. When **In Demand** 157

12. Misconceptions **About The Business** 159

13. Final **Thoughts** 165

Why **Write This Book?**

Ispeak all over the United States and Canada on the subject of modeling. The audience is usually filled with young teenagers and adults. When I look out into the audience, I see so many faces with so much hope and so many dreams in their eyes. Their eagerness is necessary. This is not an easy business to get into. Next to those hopeful faces, I see a parent whose face is concerned, worried, and seems to be saying, "I don't care about your biography or the fabulous supermodels you made. **I just want to know how I can get my kid into this business, and, please, without it costing me a fortune.**" Of course, they have other concerns, but this question usually makes it or breaks it for their child's dreams.

For those reasons, I decided to write a to-the-point guidebook. **My main intention was to envision myself as a mom in mid-America.** "My youngest child is now a teenager and wants more than ever to be a model. I know my child is tall and skinny, and to me, beautiful. I just don't know a thing about the modeling business or anyone in it. Plus, my teenager has never been far from home. On top of all of that, I have five other kids to support and how the heck am I going to get my teenager into the business and pay for it?

This book may not cover every aspect of what the business is about, or everything you can expect once you get representation, but

I will share tidbits about these things along the way. **This book is mainly about the nuts and bolts of getting young hopefuls into modeling.**

There are only a few entryways I recommend for models to get into the business safely and successfully. **The safest and most successful ways are contacting agencies directly; entering a legitimate contest involving a prestigious and reputable client, magazine, or agency; or going to a reputable, established model convention where you have the opportunity to meet many different types of agents in one shot.** I strongly believe if you read this book thoroughly and follow through on my advice, you will without a doubt maximize your chances of getting signed by an agency to start your career as a model.

The great thing about modeling is that there are many different levels of modeling, just like any other business. You can use modeling to supplement your college education. You can model and have a primary job with flexibility. You can model and have a family. You can model and make it your main priority. You can model and aim to be the best.

It's a dream business with many people wishing to become a model and few getting the chance. You have to pull your head out of the clouds and get down to business if you want to make your your dreams come true.

: C h a p t e r 1 :
Where **Do Hopefuls Start?**

Y ou have to start with you! **You are the product, and you can't go to market until the product is right, tried, tested and ready for sale.** You could go to "market," meaning you could go see agencies without being ready, BUT you could potentially save thousands and thousands of dollars by making sure you are "ready for market" before you even walk into an agency. If you have had the luck of contact with a reputable and professional scouting convention or have been scouted by an agency, **I recommend that you read this book thoroughly to make sure you maximize your opportunities.** This is important because it could be your best shot ever, and just because they are interested does NOT mean they are 100% sold. You have to be fully prepared to ensure positive responses.

We will go through this process of getting you, the product, as ready as possible. It is a worthwhile process and will save you time and money in the long run. Some of you will think, "But this process is taking up precious time that I could be using to contact agencies!" Trust me, nothing is farther from the truth. For agencies, nothing is worse than meeting someone who is unprepared or has spent thousands of dollars on a portfolio that is not even close to what works for fashion. **If you don't do it right from the beginning, you could severely limit your opportunities of getting an agency. If you do get an agency and are not prepared, your agency will tell you some-**

where down the line to do these things. Thus, you will have lost time and money.

Again, you are the product in the world of modeling. It is based first on your looks and second on your personality. **Once your look is deemed appropriate, your personality becomes paramount.** Always build your base strong. It's a long climb up, and if you fall, you want to make sure you have something secure to land on.

If your ambitions are high, meaning you want to become a supermodel, it is just as hard to become a supermodel as it is to become a superstar like Tom Cruise in the film business. It will take time and education as well as cost you physically, mentally, emotionally and financially. You will have to want to model more than anything. **The competition is fierce.** There are over one hundred and ninety countries of men and women in the world wanting to be top models. Some of them are coming from harsh situations, such as extreme poverty, and they will do whatever it takes to upgrade their situation in life. I heard a top agent in New York City say, "I would love to see an American supermodel, but the models from Brazil and Russia work so much harder and diligently to make it. The U.S.A. is a very spoiled country."

The U.S.A. is also a very lucky country. Perhaps things do come easier to us than if we were born elsewhere. Still,the majority of our success stories are based on hard work and perseverance. If you think it's going to be easy to make it to the supermodel level, think again. Do you think that if you had average grades and chose to go to your local community college that you would have an easy road to your dream of running Harvard's top-rated medical school? Do you think if you are at a job, cop an attitude, are impolite and lazy that you will be promoted? **You must view modeling as a business, and you must look at it like any other business. Every business costs money, every business takes time, and every business involves education, experience, and a positive attitude to make it successful.**

For example, if you open a t-shirt shop in a small town, and think that you could be the best t-shirt shop in all of America, what do you think t-shirt manufacturers are going to do? Will they say, "Oh, we believe you are going to be the best. Here, have our t-shirts for your shop free. Here, have a long line of credit with us for free, even though you haven't given us one valid reason to believe you are going to be better than all the other t-shirt shops in the country. Wow, you are it. We know you will be the best." Now, you and I know that wouldn't happen, so why would it happen in modeling?

You have to be prepared to prove that you, the product, are ready for the fashion industry. You will have to prove that you have what it takes and can make it in modeling. **Modeling doesn't have to prove anything to you until you are what it wants.**

The **Modeling Business**
The Big Picture

Clients book models to advertise their products. In fashion that essentially means clothing, cosmetics, toiletries, jewelry and hair care. There are other types of advertising that use fashion models, but the main bulk of business comes from these areas. Fashion clients want beautiful people. Consumers who buy fashion products respond to advertising that emanates beauty, style and fabulous in-shape figures.

Models need agencies for several reasons. One, agencies do the footwork for the models by tracking down clients and researching if they are reputable as well as accountable for payment. Two, agencies represent many models and have a vast amount of knowledge and history with working models to share with models entering the market. Three, agencies are skilled at developing new faces and are usually networked with other agencies to help promote models' careers outward and upward to other markets and clients.

Clients prefer to work with agencies. Agencies take care of selecting and developing the models; they represent a large group of models for the clients to choose from; they act as a mediator for problems; they take care of billing; and due to the large amount of experience agencies have, they can help make suggestions to clients as well. The majority of clients do not have the time or money to handle solicitations from individual models. Agencies make the whole process much easier for them.

Agencies handle many models. Agencies can pick and choose who they want to represent, and because they usually represent more than one model, they choose to work with reputable models who fit the criteria and treat others in a pleasant, professional manner. **No matter how beautiful from the outside, agencies won't represent someone who is mean, rude, unprofessional and tacky.**

DEFINITIONS

Here are some commonly used phrases. I will also give you definitions along the way so you are not overwhelmed with too much terminology until you need it.

COUTURE, HIGH END:

This is the designer look. It is what you see in magazines such as *Vogue, Men's Italian Vogue, Harper's Bazaar, W*, designers such as Giorgio Armani, Calvin Klein, Donna Karan, Versace, Dolce Gabbana, Gucci, Prada, and high end department stores such as Barney's and Neiman Marcus. The models in this arena tend to be more unique and visually impactful than a basic catalogue model. Think super, unbelievably gorgeous; or a strong, geometric look that could be taken as ugly or beautiful, dependent upon whose view it is.

EDITORIAL:

Editorial has two definitions in the fashion industry. For all markets, "editorial" is the pages (commonly called "tearsheets") in a magazine that tell a story with different fashion outfits. For example, the middle pages of *Vogue* or *GQ.* **Models aspire to book editorial to fill their model photo albums, which are called "portfolios".** Editorial in your portfolio is the stamp of approval that you are a working model. **In the bigger fashion markets, such as New York and Paris, "editorial" stands for the look of a model that is couture and high end.** If an agent says to you, "your look is editorial," they mean you have the potential to book the high end magazines, designers and clients.

E DGY:

Think funkier, not typically styled. **A little more off the beaten track, more city stylization, modern, and not 100% classic.** An example of "classic"would be a typical, stylized short men's hair cut, such as you may see in a department store catalogue. On the other hand, if you saw a young male model with a shaved head or a Beatles' styled haircut, the model would be considered "edgy". This gives the model a bit more of a unique style so that the model transcends normal and traditional looks.

F ASHION/ CATALOGUE:

If a model is referred to as a "fashion/catalogue" look, this is the typical, good-looking mass America look. It is what you see in Abercrombie & Fitch, *Marie Claire, Glamour,* department stores such as Dillards, JC Penney, Rich's, and Macy's. You also see it in advertising such as Neutrogena,

Salon Selectives, and Gillette Mach 3 Razors. For North America, it tends to be a beautiful person that the general public can relate to -- not too threatening or too unique, but still very good looking.

ETHNICITY:

Colors of skin other than white Caucasian. **Be aware the preferred skin color of models changes per country, as the advertisers' mainstream consumers change to different ethnic origins.** Thankfully, skin colors of all types are being used in the U.S.A. This is not the case in all countries, as the demographics for their buyers are different. **For example, Italy doesn't book a lot of black models.** Then again, there aren't many black consumers living in Italy. When choosing where you want to model, you must be conscious of what your skin and hair color are in regard to the country's consumer demographics.

Taking **Your Self-Assessment**

I**can't stress enough how important it is to take a self-assessment.** You are the product. If you take the time to make the product the best you can, you will do so much better when you go out into the modeling industry. **Put your investment in YOU first.** By looking at yourself how the fashion industry will look at you, you will see what you need to work on. After you have worked on whatever areas need help, then you can go forward into the modeling industry. There is nothing worse than you, the product, not being ready and prepared. **If you don't prep yourself, you run a higher risk of going out into the business and not getting the results you want.** Botched up results cost you money and time. I know I keep hyping on this point, but it is the point that so many potential models disregard. It saddens me to see you lowering your chances of succeeding in this wonderful and interesting industry.

I want to make one side note here. You can do all the right things and be blessed enough to get signed by a good agency, begin photo shoots and other investments, to find out you are still not being marketed correctly. This happens. **Agencies do their best to market you in the right direction, but sometimes it doesn't come together in the form of bookings.** So, if you're not booking jobs, your agency may need to alter some things to get your career in the right direction. Why not lessen the chance of this happening from the beginning? Let's start from the top and work our way down - literally.

The **Outer You**

A: THINK NATURAL

Natural works best. Let the professionals -- the agents and all the creative people -- figure out which way to take you because they know what sells. If agents can't see you as natural as possible, it's difficult for them to assess what you really look like and what direction is best for you.

Make yourself as clean as a canvas before an artist starts a painting. Think of this scenario: Calvin Klein is having a casting. You, along with four hundred other models in New York City, fall into the realm of what he is looking for. Calvin is looking for a beautiful female model with great skin, an interesting ethereal beauty that represents an all-American appeal. Castings can be this broadly descriptive.

In your opinion, you look your best with eyeliner, a bit of eyeshadow and a darker lipstick, and you don't leave the house without them. **You have looked at the Calvin Klein ads and you have even had people comment that you look like a model in a Calvin Klein ad.** For the casting, you decide to make yourself up just like the model in his last campaign. You feel very self-assured that you have a strong chance of booking this casting.

Calvin, on the other hand, the artist and creator of the advertising, has decided to go in a completely different direction than his last campaign. He is envisioning a model with no make-up, very matte, and in all neutral colors. Then, you walk in with your preconceived notion of what he wants. **Is he going to book you? It's going to be pretty hard because he can't even envision you past the eyeliner, the eye shadow and the lipstick to see what you really look like.**

I know all of the females out there are aghast. From all the pictures of models in magazines, it is easy to assume they are always wearing make-up when this could not be further from the truth. Sometimes for show castings and other specific castings they are, but overall, NO. **You must create the cleanest canvas possible so that the artist, the creator, can draw on you.**

If you choose to be the artist, then you lose the opportunity to get the booking. You are a model. A model, in a sense, is a walking and talking mannequin -- just like the mannequins you see in the stores with clothes styled a certain way so that you, the buyer, can visualize an outfit on yourself and decide if the style if right for you. The only difference is that you bring along your wonderful and unique personality. How can anyone decide if you are right for an advertisement or clothing line if they can't see you in the most natural state? Does a mannequin not arrive at the store neutral, with nothing on it? Then, arriving as natural as possible will work best for you as well.

B: YOUR HAIR

No matter what type of hair you have, it must be healthy, soft and shiny. I recommend you check out products that increase the health of your hair, as well as products specifically used to create luster and shine. Also, consider buying a health food store multi-vitamin, which helps your hair get the vitamins and minerals it needs to be its vibrant best. And remember our first lesson, natural is best.

Don't go for excessive, edgy haircuts in the beginning. Most of you will get your start in smaller markets. In smaller markets, an edgy haircut will severely hurt you. For example, how many buyers in Oklahoma City can relate to an edgy, chopped-up haircut? Consumers tend to relate to models that are a mirror reflection of their own lifestyle or the lifestyle they wish to acquire. **You have to think, "Do the consumers in this market relate to edgy, cool and hip?" In Oklahoma City, probably not.** An excessive, edgy haircut could hurt your booking potential. Sure, there might be a few bookings for that look, but overall you just cut yourself out of the market.

If your market is Los Angeles or New York, your agent may want to pull you into an edgy cut. These are markets where that look is more marketable, as buyers can envision themselves in the edgier image. So, in the beginning, the best piece of advice is to keep it simple with maybe just a bit of edge, if any.

Have a flexible haircut. Overall, agents want to see hair not too long. Women, if you have hair below the nipple, you are covering up the clothes and the clothes is what the client is trying to sell -- not your hair.

FOR WOMEN:

"Long" in most markets is somewhere between above the nipple and below the collarbone. If you insist on wearing your hair longer than your breasts, then you will have fewer booking options. Clients don't want to book a model if they always have to put the hair behind the shoulder. They will just book another model with a more flexible haircut.

I recommend a cut somewhere between one inch below the collarbone to just touching the shoulder. Fringed layers around the face work well because they allow the client the flexibility to make your hair appear different lengths and show off different styles. The versatility of this type of cut equates back to you in higher earnings because you relate to more buyers. **When looking through magazines, search for the most consistent haircuts on models similar to yourself. That is probably a good indication of where you should start.**

I have seen some models have very short, extreme haircuts. This type of cut can be an entryway into editorial and high end clients. This extreme look screams "city" and you have to have the right face for this type of haircut. Still, I recommend you keep your hair longer until an agent makes the decision towards an edgy haircut. If you are set on having super short hair, first go try on some wigs and see how you look. **To have a very short haircut, I believe you either have to have an overwhelmingly stunning, gorgeous face, or your bone struc-**

ture has to have great geometric balance and dimensions that make your face as unique as the cut.

Short bangs can be limiting. Bangs cut straight across the eyebrow can be seen as one-dimensional, because the client can't do much else with them. Again, there are models that have bangs that use this look as an entryway into editorial. It also can appeal to clients as an "Asian" or "city" look. I actually like bangs but I feel it is important that they are longer, preferably to the nose, and textured, so that they can be combed into the hair if a client prefers it that way. **Again, there are always exceptions, but letting your agency make the decision with you is always best because agencies know their clients far better than you do.**

Clients like to use models with versatile haircuts. Whether your hair is long or short, it must be flexible and easily styled in several variations. Too long can be an issue as much as too short. **If your hair is so short that the client can do nothing else with it, then they may feel you have a "mono look."** This means your look is the same in every picture. To a client, this says you are only marketable to one type of consumer – someone with your look, your haircut, and only in your style. But, as I pointed out before, severe, short haircuts can work in larger, editorial markets to jump start a model's career by potentially making the model more unique than the average model in the market. Overall, it is the rare few that have more success with a severe, short haircut.

FOR MEN:

I don't recommend super long hair for men -- any length below the chin. There are some male models who start their careers with long hair and if you are absolutely fabulous with long hair, then maybe you should do the same; however, you must remember that long hair has its limitations. **Most long-haired male models cut their hair after a couple of years** because the majority of clients book men with hair that is like the majority of the male population.

White men with curly hair have a look that usually does not work as it represents a small percentage of the buying public. Again, there is a very small percentage that make curly hair work. **Most of the male models I have represented with curly hair have gotten it relaxed or straightened so that they can attain a greater number of bookings.** Relaxing the hair does not mean your hair has to always be worn straight. It just makes it easier to wear straight by softening the curl.

Some men shave their heads. If you are young, this would only be a short-term look as you are limiting the number of bookings available to you. Although, having a shaved head could be your entryway in because some high fashion magazines like to book this edgy look into their editorial pages. Shaving your head is a decision that should definitely be left up to your agency. How many young men have shaved heads? Are they buying a lot of fashion or are young men with hair? Clients want to appeal to more buyers, and young men with hair are buying more.

Men in their 30's or older with a shaved head or are balding can definitely have careers. Why? Even though some men wish they had more hair, they don't. We are living in a world where celebrities, such as Bruce Willis, are considered gorgeous and sexy with little to no hair. This, combined with the natural fact that many men lose their hair, has helped bald heads become a more marketable look for this age range.

For the most flexibility for booking opportunities, men should have their bangs a bit longer, where the hair touches the nose, and the side length is slightly over the ears and short in the back. If your hair is full and healthy, this type of hair style can be combed conservatively, it can be tousled to look sexy, it can be combed to one side or the other, or it can be worn straight back. It allows for more options for the client which equates to more buyers for the client and more bookings for you. Be sure in advance that your hair is not thin. Thin hair needs to stay short to look fuller.

A lot of male models wear their hair quite short as well. This does not mean the hair is one-eighth of an inch to the scalp. The hair usually is at least an inch or two in length and can be varied somewhat.

FOR BLACKS:

If you have photos with your hair in different styles (home family photos are fine), bring them when seeing agencies. Sometimes models do look better with extensions or their hair relaxed. It's best to show your hair au natural and bring along other photo options so the agents can make a good judgment call on what is best for you. **I have yet to see a model make it to great lengths with braids or dreads,** so please skip these two options from the beginning.

FOR BLONDES:

It is best to get your hair color to the lowest maintenance level possible. That means natural blonde or highlights in different shades of light to dark that are not extreme variations from your roots. Then when your hair grows out, the clients will not see a block of blonde followed by a darker block of your natural hair color near the roots. I have seen way too many potential models with over-processed blonde hair. Not only does it look unhealthy, it also looks unnatural and that stops an agent from the get-go because the agent figures this is how you want to look. Plus, the agent realizes the process of getting you back to a natural color could take too much time. **If your hair is processed too light blonde or too unnatural, it's best you go through the process to naturalize it now before trying to secure an agency.**

A piece of advice to processed blondes: Make sure you can do it yourself. What if your hairdresser is the only one who can do it? What do you going to do when you are in Asia for eight weeks? Or Milan? Are you going to trust someone else to do it? What if they mess up? That is why I stress the lowest maintenance blonde color at the beginning. If your New York agency chooses to make you a platinum blonde and you are booking *Harper's Bazaar,* then they will make sure to keep it the right color with the right hair stylists wherever you travel. At the beginning, you have to be responsible for you, and how are you going to maintain it if you are not near your stylist? Think ahead.

FOR CURLY-HAIRED WOMEN:

You want to make sure you show agents your hair both curly and straight. Curly-haired models work, but most clients prefer straight because the majority of people in the world have straight hair. This doesn't mean your curly hair is a liability. Curly hair is actually an asset because clients like the flexibility. You just want to make sure a client knows you can wear your hair both curly and straight.

Most curly-haired women find it hard to blow-dry their hair straight without damaging it. **I recommend working with a hair professional to learn the quickest and healthiest way to straighten your hair.** I have seen some curly-haired models have up to 80% of their bookings request straight hair. That's a lot of straightening. If your agency foresees many of your bookings requesting straight hair, make sure it doesn't harm your hair. Some curly-haired models choose to get it relaxed, but not to the point of completely losing the curl.

Curly hair must not look frizzy, dried out or dull. Make sure you invest in products that keep your hair looking beautiful and curly. When straightening your hair make sure to buy a good straightening iron that keeps it looking healthy and shiny with no frizziness.

BE INVOLVED IN DECISIONS ABOUT YOUR HAIR:

Agents know a lot but, in truth, you "hire" an agency to work for you. You are a team and working together is

always best to optimize your results. I have had models who are blonde tell me they are going to become a brunette, and I can't fathom it for the life of me. Then, they show me a picture in a wig and they look fabulous. We agents don't always have all the answers.

Brunettes work more. More of the world is brunette, but that doesn't mean everyone should go brunette. Even if the world is a majority of brunettes, there are many blondes and redheads. And on top of that, blondes and redheads have a certain mystique that will always sell.

It's best to make the decision with your agency. I usually only change a model's hair color when I have to look at why they aren't working. Sometimes a model's face just warrants a different hair color for them to be that much more spectacular and thus, more marketable.

I recently made a redhead a brunette because she had more interest from Asian markets than any other markets. She has a beautiful oval face,and her eyes slightly slant up even though she is not of Asian descent at all. Her face is very marketable in Asia, but her natural red hair is not. All the interested agencies asked if she would color her hair brown because the Asian demographics have a stronghold of dark-haired consumers. I didn't make the decision alone. She had to be involved in the process, obviously, because it's her hair, and also because she had to like the idea. If she didn't like the idea and we went ahead anyway, she wouldn't be able to sell the image to clients because her negative attitude would go along with it.

Agents are not fortunetellers. We can't give you guarantees that something will definitely work. We are only doing our best from what we know about our clients and from our previous experience with other models. Keep in mind that we want it to work. If it doesn't work, we don't make money and neither do you. This is a business, and like any other business, it is about making money.

C: YOUR FACE

Is there a certain type of face that only works in our business? Not really, but there are certain things that deter agents from signing models. Let's go through what agents look for and you will see what they don't want as well.

HEALTHY, BEAUTIFUL SKIN:

It's a must. **Your skin has to be healthy, beautiful and acne free.** Clients will cover up a blemish or two, but they prefer blemish-free skin. Clear skin is less complicated, the client doesn't have to touch up the photos, and there are many models with perfect skin to choose from. So, it's best to make your skin a priority now.

Do you have acne? Look at your diet first. It's the most healthy, practical and economical first step. The first question I ask a newcomer with acne is, "Do you take a health food store multi-vitamin?" More than three-quarters of the time the response is "no". Your skin will react if you are not eating healthy. I recommend health food store multi-vitamins because my naturopathic doctor believes the generic vitamins sold in regular stores are not as absorbable.

Always take your vitamins with food or after food. If you take vitamins on an empty stomach, they can make you nauseous. I prefer to take mine at night after dinner as I am usually not as active then and the vitamins sit in my system for a longer time. For women, I stress a calcium with magnesium supplement for your long-term bone health, and my doctor recommends taking these at night as well for absorption. My calcium also has zinc which is noted to be very good for the skin. The condition of your skin will improve with the proper vitamins and minerals.

Maintaining a good, healthy diet with lots of vegetables and fruits is a must. Try to stay away from fried foods. For young people, I think it's ludicrous to expect them to eat only healthy foods with all the fast food and chemical-laden foods that are out there. **If you have acne, you have to pinpoint why it is happening.** And by looking at your diet, and noting what you eat, you can try deleting certain items one at a time for a week or so, and see if your skin gets better. Most models note either fried foods or dairy as the biggest culprits. If dairy appears to be the culprit, you may be dealing with food allergies. To find out if you have food allergies, try either an allergist, a naturopathic doctor, or an acupuncturist.

EXAMINE HOW CLEAN YOU KEEP YOUR FACE:

✦ Are you using a cleanser that helps your skin be its best? There are numerous, inexpensive over the counter prod-

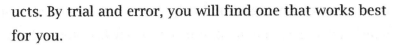

ucts. By trial and error, you will find one that works best for you.

✦ Do you rinse the cleanser off your face thoroughly? Dermatologists recommend splashing your face with lukewarm water twenty times.

✦ Do you change your facial towel often? It can collect dirt and bacteria that you do not need to rub back into your skin while drying your face.

✦ Do you lightly exfoliate your skin? Dead skin cells can build up in pores and irritate your skin.

✦ If you have acne, do you use any over-the-counter remedies? Besides cleansers, there are numerous acne remedies available.

✦ Do you keep your hands off your face? Your hands may appear clean but are really quite dirty, and every time you touch your face, you are pushing dirt and grease right into your pores.

✦ Do you wear your hair away from your face at night and change your pillowcase often? Your hair's natural oils can get on your skin and on your pillowcase.

✦ Are your hair products helping your skin? Your hair products may be keeping your hair healthy and shiny and, at the same time, it may be causing acne on your face.

If you said "no" to any of these, try to change these habits first and see if it helps.

If you still have skin problems, and I mean anything from blackheads to lots of tiny bumps or plain old acne on your

face, you need professional help. In our business, "acne problems" range from a daily pimple or weekly breakouts. If you fit in this category, and you've tried all my previous suggestions to no avail, then you need to make an appointment with a dermatologist. Make sure to discuss any acne scarring with your dermatologist. There are simple medical remedies to diminish scarring, such as light chemical peels.

Clear, healthy skin is imperative in our business. The normal female excuse of "it's that time of the month" or the male excuse of "it's from shaving" will not work. Some clients are okay with a few blemishes, but there are enough clients out there that are not. Once again, there are enough models out there with perfectly clear skin that a client can book instead of you. That alone is reason enough to clear up your skin.

If you are older, you need to take a serious look at what time has done to your skin. Have you had too much sun? If so, that means you have to stay out of the sun and protect your skin from the sun with good SPF protection. If your skin looks older than your age, you may need to change your eating habits to help get your skin healthier. You may need to take a health food store multi-vitamin. You may need to get facial peels or Retin-A through a dermatologist.

Many older models get peels to counteract the aging process, as well as light scarring. Most models get a glycolic acid peel, which usually costs under $80 per application. This process involves a light amount of glycolic acid that is swabbed on your skin, which lightly burns off the top layer or two. This peel allows for light lines and scarring to be diminished by revealing younger looking, healthier new skin. Immediately after the procedure, your skin will have a light redness. The redness dissipates within a couple hours. Your face will begin to lightly peel dry skin off within two to three days. A week later, you can already tell that your skin looks better. I have seen it do wonders for my own skin and for models as well. You may have to go through as many as ten peels to get your skin in good shape. If you have worse acne scars, you may need to look into more serious peels, which range from $400 and up.

Stay out of the sun. Whether you are light or olive skinned, nothing will destroy your face and career quicker than too much sun. In the long run, it makes you look wrinkled like hard leather and it ages you tremendously. In the short run, you develop premature lines around the eyes and between the mouth and nose -- **these two areas are places that all agents look for signs of aging.** Remember, our industry is based on the youth factor.

Please keep in mind that agents usually take on models that have long term potential. I know staying out of the sun is a hard one for some of you. I look better with sun but then again, I am not a model. **All of us would be smarter and healthier to stay out of the sun to ensure our skin looks better longer.**

I run into several situations with young hopefuls and tanning. One scenario is where potential Caucasian models will tell me they can get tanner if they need to be. This happens to me quite often in the South. I have to stress to young hopefuls that the majority of markets want a model to be as light skinned as possible. The exceptions to this rule are Miami Beach, Cape Town in South Africa and sometimes Los Angeles.

The other situation arises when I view potential candidates at a model convention. A fabulous young face walks out onto the runway so over-tanned and you hear all the agents quietly groan. The agents really don't know what this young hopeful is thinking. If you are considering this option, think again. **Look through the magazines. There lies your answer. How many over-tanned models do you really see?**

If you feel a bit of sun makes you look better, just do it in small degrees and with good SPF protection, or try the self-tanning products that look natural. **Our business emphasizes youth, health and beauty.** The sun will take all three away from you very quickly.

If you have scars on your face or visibly important areas of your body, you want to work beforehand on minimizing them. For light facial scars, you can get facial peels, as described above. **Thankfully, for both face and body, there are some wonderful, inexpensive scar diminishing products on the market.** Some of the products are a pure silicone sheeting that smoothes, and flattens scars, restoring skin to a more normal texture and color.

Here are some suggestions in using silicone sheeting products. Cut the sheet to the size of the scar and wear it at night. Many models find it difficult to keep the sheet in place on some parts of the face with the tape provided. You may have to get stickier stay-on tape to make it work. Some models have used the new silicone products in gel form that are designed to do the same thing but must be applied up to 4 times a day. You cannot speed up the process by wearing these products all day. The skin needs to breathe so it can fully regenerate. To give you an idea of how well it works, **I have had models wear the silicone sheet on a chicken pox scar and six weeks later the chicken pox scar is virtually undetectable.**

If peels or products don't work, you may need to go to a plastic surgeon and discuss other options to remove the scar. I once represented a young model with a strong scar in the middle of her forehead. She went to a plastic surgeon who said it would cost approximately $3,000 to make her scar less noticeable. She was hesitant to spend the money to have it removed when, in truth, the scar really didn't bother her much. Plus, her parents viewed it as a very large investment to put into a business with no guarantees. I told her that she would have to make the choice herself, as agents cannot professionally make the decision for her. She argued that it could be covered with heavy make-up, or touched up in Photo Shop on the computer. I agreed. **The scar could be covered or touched up, but I countered that most clients simply wouldn't deal with it, and would go ahead and book a model without a scar in the middle of the forehead.**

This model had lots of potential. If she had the scar removed for $3,000, as a new model she would make that money back in less than three days of catalogue bookings. No, there were no guarantees that the removal of the scar would make her career. **She had to decide if she wanted to model as a career and optimize her booking potential or not.** She chose to have it done.

That year, she worked in Los Angeles, as well as her smaller home market, and more than easily covered her investment.

If you have moles on your face, you probably don't have much to worry about. It will, of course, depend on how big, how dark and how many you have. **The Asian markets are quite particular about moles,** and if you have many, or even a few well-defined ones on your face or body, they may not accept you for work unless you are a supermodel. Hopefully, that will change with time. Perfect, flawless skin is one of the most important beauty traits in Asian culture.

I have only once told a model to consider having a mole removed. She had absolutely none on her entire face. Then, she had one very dark, small, but still defined mole in the middle of her chin about an inch below her bottom lip. She was not very tall but absolutely perfect for the Asian markets, with the exception of the mole. I told her that if the mole could be removed inexpensively and did not leave a scar, it could mean the difference of thousands and thousands of potential dollars to her in the Asian markets. Since her height would make her compete with much taller couture women in larger markets, I felt it was best to let her know how the markets that are open to shorter models would feel, particularly Asia. The point is to make money, and for that reason alone, I made her aware of this.

If you have baby fat on your face, meaning that your cheeks are very chubby or you have a slight double chin, it can effect your options in the modeling industry. If you are a teenager, you will most likely grow out of this phase. It's baby

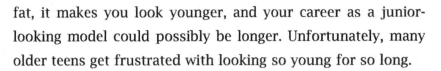

fat, it makes you look younger, and your career as a junior-looking model could possibly be longer. Unfortunately, many older teens get frustrated with looking so young for so long.

Looking a certain age can help determine your earnings. For example, if you are a fifteen-year-old female model but you look twenty-three on film, you are in the range of a larger buying public than your own age range and you will have more opportunities to work. In comparison, if you photograph younger than your fifteen years, you could possibly have less work available to you. Thirteen to fifteen-year-olds don't buy as many things as someone who looks twenty-three; therefore, your work would be less until you look older.

I feel a little baby fat is just fine because it lengthens your career. Maybe the beginning of your career will be slower, but it probably will be in tune with the rest of your life at that moment. Whereas, if you look far older than your fifteen years, you most likely will look even older at twenty-one years of age; therefore, your career could be shorter. On another note, if you were looking your age at fifteen, could you even realistically work full-time? **Even with all these rationalizations, teens that look really young can still get discouraged.**

I have the blessing of representing a beautiful male teen. I have represented him since he was fifteen-years-old. He always had the option to travel anytime of the year because he could be home-schooled by his mother who could travel with him. In the beginning, I brought up the fact that the baby fat on his face would be an issue and he would have to wait it out. Still, he and his mom urged me to try. For two and a half years he kept getting turned down over and over by big market agents. **They said his face was too full and young and they wanted to watch him develop as he got older.** His mother took this feedback negatively. They were frustrated because they lived in a market where there really wasn't a teen/junior client base. Understandably, they wanted to go somewhere else. As with most teens, I felt pretty assured it was just a matter of time and his face would slim out as he grew up, and he would look a bit older and more marketable.

His baby fat came off by his senior year in high school. He first decided to finish out his senior year, which made sense since graduation was so near. He then modeled in Munich his first summer out, followed by Athens and then Milan. **He realized that my initial assumptions were right. There was no reason to worry, and he should have been more patient during those early years.** In some cases, there is nothing much an agent can do until the excess baby fat comes off.

If your baby fat doesn't trim off as you get older, or you are already older, you may need to lose five or seven pounds and see if it helps. This can only be done if your frame can handle the loss of the weight. If you naturally have a round face, it may make you look heavier overall. To make it to certain levels in fashion modeling, with the exception of plus modeling, you don't want to appear heavier. If you have this problem, it may mean you will have to be slightly slimmer than your same height counterparts. Make sure to lose weight in a healthy manner. Staying healthy is just as important as staying slim to maximize your booking options.

There is one market that definitely doesn't mind a little baby fat. That is Hollywood. Having baby fat can make you look younger. If you look younger than your real age, you can handle difficult roles with maturity, but still look young enough for the part.

EYES

If your eyes are close together, this can be considered problematic in the modeling industry. On film, people with close set eyes often appear cross-eyed. Depending on the overall geometry of your face, it either works or it doesn't. I met a young hopeful from the Los Angeles area when I was scouting at a convention. From the runway, she looked spectacular, very editorial and stunning. When standing right in front of me, her eyes seemed a bit close together. I asked her to pluck her eyebrows a bit more in the middle bridge area to give the illusion of wider set eyes. She also needed to come down about twelve pounds in order to be a couture model. **As she dropped the weight and sent me snapshots, it was incredible how her eyes were balancing out with her cheekbones coming out.** Yes, her eyes were still closer together than the average person, but I thought it looked very cool. That doesn't mean everyone else will think her eyes are cool, but my believing in her is the first important step. **Our industry has a saying: "All you need is one good agent to believe in you."**

Women with close set eyes should discuss this with the make-up artist before a photo shoot. One would assume a professional make-up artists will notice this on their own, but they are not always assessing the geometry of faces. Let them know so they don't do anything that would exaggerate it further. Also learn how to apply eye make-up to lessen this issue as well. Any top of the line make-up line (for example, Chanel) usually has a make-up artist at their sales counter that can teach you a few tricks to give the illusion of wider set eyes.

For men with close set eyes, I always take a good look at their eyebrows. Sometimes, their eyebrows can be plucked just a bit in the middle bridge area. By doing this, it sometimes helps create eyes that appear further set apart. Just make sure to not over do it. Your brows should never be plucked further back than in perfect alignment with a line vertically straight up beginning next to the side of your nose.

EYEBROWS

Natural is the key. That doesn't mean just let them be and not shape them. It means make them appear natural if you pluck them differently than what you were born with.

For men, don't touch your eyebrows unless you have the uni-brow, or they are super thick. Uni-brow means the hair goes from one eyebrow then across the bridge of the nose to the other eyebrow making one long brow. If you have a uni-brow, it's important that you pluck in the middle but not too much. Keep in mind again, that if a pencil is right next to the side of your nose positioned vertically upward, that is the point where your eyebrows should begin.

For women, the majority of the time I see eyebrows that are over-plucked. You look younger with thicker eyebrows.

Our business is built on the youth factor. Women should pluck any stray hairs from across the bridge of their nose, as noted above. Never pluck hairs from the top of the natural line of the brow. It is one of the most common mistakes I see. Never pluck hairs from below the natural line of the brow until just after the point where the outside line of the black pupil is vertically lined up to the brow. From this point on, the brow can be shaped slimmer if preferred. Make sure not to pluck hairs from the end of the eyebrow causing the brow line to appear shorter. Only pluck hairs at the end if the entire line is further out than a pencil slanted up from the lower side of the nose through the tip of the outer edge of the eye to the brow. **I spend more time waiting for models to repair over-plucked eyebrows than anything. Don't do it.**

I know it is hard to believe this is true. You look at editorial after editorial in the high end magazines with female models with very thin eyebrows, and sometimes no eyebrows at all. I can guarantee you that the majority of models start out with nice, healthy, thicker eyebrows. **Let the agents, the artists, decide what direction to take your eyebrows so that your bookings are maximized, instead of minimized right from the beginning.**

For super light eyebrow hair, just let it be until an agent makes a judgment call on it. Sometimes, the super light brow works great, especially for high end editorial. Sometimes agents will have you slightly darken your brows so they show up better in pictures. **Please, don't ever tattoo your eyebrows.** If you have already done this, I recommend working with creams that will cover over up the tattooed brows because they are usually too dark and unnatural.

THE NOSE

Today, thankfully, many different types of noses work within reason. All agents are not perfect, and "the nose" brings me to my worst agent experience. **Years ago I had a model who everyone loved, but no one liked her nose.** I told her I couldn't tell her what to do, but she might want to consider a nose job. We envisioned this perfect nose and successful modeling career. Unfortunately, the plastic surgeon didn't do a very good job and her nose looked even worse. Most agents have a conscience and it plagued me for years. I swore I would never take another model with a nose issue. Today I am so thankful to see our business accept so many different types of noses. We have come a long way.

If your nose has been broken or has other problems that show up on film, you will need to address this. Even though all shapes are accepted today, bumps, big scars or broken bones can minimize your industry options. **Male models tend to fare better with nose imperfections than female models.**

Nose hairs should never be noticeable and should be kept plucked or trimmed out of the way.

NICE SMILE

Your smile should be nice from all angles. **This doesn't mean that your teeth have to be perfect,** but it does mean that they have to be straight enough, not too short, not too long, not too gapped, not too fangy and not too stained or yellow.

Your teeth should also look nice when your mouth is slightly parted. That may sound strange to you, but it's true. Sometimes models have perfect teeth when they smile, but when their mouth is slightly open, the teeth can look like a cartoon rabbit's where the two front teeth are more pronounced. I have known models that in person you do not notice this problem at all. Then you see their photos, and it's quite evident that it's a problem. Also, teeth that are straight but angle inward or outward can cause a problem on film. The easiest way to see if your teeth have any photographic problems is to check your home photos.

Having a basic, nice smile is simple. Practice good dental hygiene. Brush your teeth for two minutes each morning and each night. Make sure to floss very well, especially at night. Also, swishing water through your mouth for thirty seconds after every meal helps to prevent tartar build up. Keeping a hygienic mouth is smart so your breath won't offend anyone.

If your teeth are crooked or out of place, you may have to opt for braces. During your time in braces, depending on what your agent says, you will either forego modeling for awhile or realize that work will be limited. Some models get bonding to even out the length of the teeth or the overall spacing between teeth. Some models get their teeth slightly filed down if they are too long. The filing process can usually only make about an eighth to a quarter of an inch difference because if the filing went any further, it could damage essential nerves in your teeth. Still, that minimum amount can make all the difference in photos.

Many models use whitening products to make their teeth appear brighter. **If you smoke or drink coffee, please make sure to use teeth whitening products.**

I meet many hopeful candidates that overlook the teeth issue. Some people overlook their teeth because they feel they are on a time crunch with their careers. Believe me, you will save time and money by taking care of your teeth before starting your career. **At some point, if your teeth are not in good shape, you will hit a ceiling with work opportunities that is caused by the condition of your teeth.** You can shoot shots with your mouth closed, and there are jobs that don't require good teeth and smiles. But overall, what catalogue can you name where the models aren't smiling more than half of the time? And in the long run, catalogs are the bread and butter of most models' careers.

Too much teeth. The best way to describe the look is the Cheshire Cat's teeth in *Alice In Wonderland*. The feeling of too much teeth is usually accompanied by the feeling of a larger mouth. Agents and clients feel that it overwhelms the balance of the face. This can usually be corrected by learning to smile with your mouth less open. Work to make it look natural and not contrived. Sometimes, a smile appears too big due to the length of the teeth. In this case, try to learn to smile with your lips less open, over your gums and over some of your teeth. If that doesn't work, you can resort to asking your dentist to file the length of your teeth a bit. Again, they cannot file much, but sometimes it can make all the difference.

THE LIPS

It is rare that a person can't model due to the shape of his or her lips. Some agents do not like thin upper lips. For me, it depends on how the lip size fits with the overall face. I personally don't recommend plastic surgery or collagen injections. There are over-the-counter remedies that plump up the lips, but that is only a short-term remedy. At some point, during a full day booking, the truth will show up.

If your lips are naturally slim, work on making them appear naturally fuller. A lot of times your lips really aren't as thin as you think they are. I meet many new hopefuls who show their stressful emotions through their mouths. They tighten their mouths up when they are nervous, and that makes their lips appear thinner. Sometimes I meet models who have had braces. I immediately see them compensating their lips by tightening up their mouths, as if they are still trying to cover up their braces with their lips. Usually, once I point this out, they are able to loosen up their mouths and their lips go back to their natural, fuller shape.

Please, be careful using lip liner to enhance your lips. Be subtle. It's very obvious when you overdraw your lips. Never ever have a lip line tattooed around your mouth. I have only seen it a couple of times, but it looks horrible. Clients don't always want a lipstick look for all jobs. Natural is always better.

You will be surprised at what you can teach your fabulous lips to do. Mouth muscles are really quite enterprising. Look at magazines and practice how models use their mouths in shots.

With time and practice, you will learn to work your mouth to where it truly looks fuller. The real toughie with thinner lips is learning to create a smile that does not lose your upper lip completely. It can be done because I have seen models with this problem overcome it.

If you have naturally slim lips at your initial photo shoots, the make-up artist may try to over-pencil your lips so they look fuller. Make sure it's not too much. The make-up artist may think no one will notice the overdrawn look in the photos, but believe me, it is usually very noticeable.

If you have full lips, you are lucky. The problem is learning how to work them. Beginning full lipped models look like they don't have control of their mouths, as one side goes up on the left, and the same side goes down on the right, or they don't shut them evenly. Sometimes models with full lips pout them too much as a photographer or some other person has told them how good it looks. You don't need to pout full lips to make them look fuller. They are already full.

There is an art to learning to work full lips. You will learn how to use them properly by practicing how full lipped models position their lips in magazines, commercials and catalogues. Some full lipped models have lips that are almost too full for most clients. They have to learn to make them look not so pronounced and appear less full. Usually keeping the mouth shut a bit tighter will work as long as it does not look uptight or stressed.

A side note to gorgeous, full lips: be careful because more times than not, make-up artists want to paint them full, dark

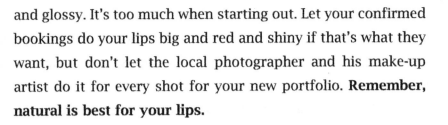
and glossy. It's too much when starting out. Let your confirmed bookings do your lips big and red and shiny if that's what they want, but don't let the local photographer and his make-up artist do it for every shot for your new portfolio. **Remember, natural is best for your lips.**

JAW LINE

If you have a weak jawbone, you must correct this. This means it is not defined separately from your neck or, another way of saying it, is that your face seems to just slide into your neck. Agents call it "the pinhead effect." If your jaw isn't well defined, you will look like a pinhead because the one-dimensional camera will not pick up a line separating your head from your neck. Most agents will not represent models with very weak jaws. Usually the problem is corrected by learning to jut your face out more.

Here is a way to learn to define your jaw better: I tell models to put their elbows on a table and put their hands under their chin as if they are posing for a childhood photo. Think Shirley Temple being cute. When they do this, their chin is out from their neck and thus defining their jaw. Then, they remove their hands and learn to *feel* what it is like to have their jaw out correctly, and voila! A stronger jaw line.

Way too many young teens push their face back into their neck and lose their jaw line because of their timidity. It is important to keep your jaw out, and to do it naturally so the agents can see that you have a defined jaw line.

For men, another contributing factor to a weak jaw is a big neck. I run into this quite often with young men who play football or are pumping iron in the gym. By intensely working out the upper body, the neck has thickened to the size of the head. To agents, these men look like pinheads. These men have to adjust their upper body workout to make this area come down to a natural size. **This usually means not working out the upper shoulder or neck area at all.** These muscle groups don't size down overnight and it could take about six months.

Ears

If your ears stick out, you will need to make a judgment call on whether they stick out too much. **Look through catalogues and magazines to see if you can find models with ears like yours.** If you find a model with ears like yours, is she famous? Does she seem to be working a lot?

Agents, more often than not, will not take on potential models if their ears stick out too far. If agents choose to sign a hopeful model with ears that stick out too much, the model usually will have a limited career because some clients will refuse to book the model. **The rationale for clients not booking models with ears sticking out too much is that the face's geometry, due to the ears, looks out of symmetry when the hair is slicked back.** Most clients like the option of having a model's hair slicked back for some of the shots.

If your ears stick out too much, stop wearing your hair behind your ears which is in no way helping the problem. Perhaps, even try a headband over your ears for some time after getting out of this habit. Some models put sticky tape behind their ears when shooting, but I have a hard time believing that works well for long.

Sometimes models with this problem will get an operation called Otoplasty. It is an operation that usually costs somewhere between $3,000 and $4,000. They make an incision behind the ear. The cartilage framework is scored with a scalpel, and then a suture is tied to increase the curvature and bring the ear closer to the head. The model is in bandages for a week or less, followed by wearing a headband at night to keep the ears in place for the duration of the healing of the sutures. Sometimes, they are then asked to continue to wear the headband for a period of time, helping the ears maintain their new appearance.

Let's face it, ears that stick out can be viewed as "cute". How often do you even notice ears unless they are very large and really, really stick out? I have represented models where I never even noticed the ear issue until I looked at a photo shoot where their hair was pulled straight back. And often, when you bring up the ear issue, a model is stunned and likes the ears just the way they are. When a model is faced with this dilemma, **I ask them to specifically find me one top model that has a major beauty/fragrance campaign, or designer campaign, or a major fashion magazine cover with ears that stick out.** Again, there lies the answer.

If you have this problem, I don't think it's imperative that you have the operation done before meeting agents. You will need to hear what agents think if your ears work or not for the business. What's important is that you should be open to hearing what agents have to say on this subject so you can optimize your career's full potential.

FACIAL HAIR

For men, at the beginning, I say "no" to facial hair unless it is for a few pictures in your book, and that should just be the five o'clock shadow look. Some guys do make it in the business with beards and/or a moustache. Overall, it's not up to you and it's a judgment call for your agency on what the trends are in the marketplace at the time. **Initially, your agent should see you clean shaven,** and you can bring along a few pictures of you with facial hair so that your agent can assess what would be best for you in the long run.

It is important to learn to shave without causing skin irritation. Sometimes clients will ask you to come with a five o'clock shadow and ask you to bring shaving cream and a razor so that you can shave half-way through the booking for a different look.

For women, facial hair is a big no-no, especially above the lip. Sometimes if it is blonde, thicker and longer, it will still show up. Some models feel they have too much hair on their cheeks and chin. Sometimes hair is growing onto your forehead from your hairline. I believe if your facial hair is dark, you definitely have to look into remedies for this. If the hair is light, you will need to make a judgment call on this or ask your agent before you start shooting pictures.

I am a big advocate of laser treatments. The procedure takes a small amount of time, anywhere from four to ten times. It is not very painful and feels like a rubber band being snapped against your skin. The laser kills the root of the hair and its effects are long-term; therefore, that saves you time and money from constantly waxing or shaving. Laser treatments work best on darker hair. Models with light hair may have to go through more treatments, and may also run into laser professionals who feel it is a waste of time. My models with light hair swear by it, but say it took a far longer time than models with dark hair. **Models who have had it done several years back swear they are still hair-free.** You don't literally end up hair-free; it just grows back lighter, shorter, softer and less noticeable. If you are thinking of having this done, please make sure to go to a licensed professional and request to see their credentials.

Make-up

If you wear make-up, learn not to wear it or make it look like you don't have any on. Be as natural as possible. "Natural" means no lip liner, lipstick or eyeliner. Agents hate potential models in make-up, especially a big "NO" for men. They can't see the real you. Think back to the Calvin Klein clean canvas scenario. Agents and clients usually want to see a model with no make-up so they can paint the canvas in their minds.

There are exceptions to this rule, including market preferences, and runway auditions for women. Make sure to ask your agency first what works in their market. Then, if clients prefer a bit of make-up, you should show your agent how you would do your make-up for castings so they can assess if it is done in the appropriate way.

Most of the time, I see young women in way too much make-up. Make-up makes you look older. If you put a thirteen-year-old in make-up, she could look as old as twenty. So, when you put a nineteen-year-old in make-up, she could look twenty-six. **You don't want to look older.** You want to look as young as possible in the fashion industry.

If you have to cover up something with make-up, try one of the heavy cover-ups for scars that match your skin's natural color and use it sparingly. It covers up blemishes well with just a dot and doesn't look like make-up if done correctly. Just put it on the blemish, not your entire face. If you insist on wearing make-up base, there is nothing worse than a make-up line along the jawline. Please be careful where you use face powder. It sinks into the pores causing shadows and can make you look pretty scary. We really don't mind if you are shiny. **Shiny looks natural, glowing and young.** If you want a natural shine, use a shine enhancer on the tops of your cheeks and a line straight down your nose so that you can have a bit more of a youthful glow.

I cannot stress the point of no make-up enough. We can't see the real you if you wear a lot of make-up. How can we tell what your potential is? When I scout models, I am painting away in my head all the types of work they can do. It's where I get to dream where the models can go. Please, don't take that away from the agents and please, don't take away your chance of getting an agency.

D: YOUR BODY

YOU HAVE TO BE IN GOOD, TONED SHAPE

I would like to believe this goes without saying in the world of fashion modeling, but it does not. Some of you are just naturally in awesome shape for our business, and some of you are not. **When I wrote the first sentence, I knew someone might take that to mean "hit the gym and pump weights." Be careful here.** Sure, weights might get you in shape, but it also might bulk you up too much. Our business is asking you to be tall, healthy and slim. Not bulky.

FOR WOMEN

Most high end couture models are not very muscular. It's not a look the designers or editorial clients want. Fashion is all about the design and the line. Clients feel too much muscle can take away from the linear silhouette of the clothing. **Female models that do more sportswear can have a stronger, muscular look** as long as it is not too much.

Clients that are exceptions to the "no bulging muscles" rule are promoting athletic clothing, equipment and resorts. Athletic models are focusing to a small sector of the business even though it is a growing sector. If you are a top notch professional at certain sports, more and more retailers, such as Nike, are expanding their clothing lines due to consumer demand, and they want to book real athletes. Still, the majority of the industry wants women to be toned, in shape, but not overly muscular. **The stomach is probably the one area where** you can get real buff, and it will always be considered sexy, no matter what category you are.

You don't want to be too skinny. If you are a tall girl from 5'8" to 5'11. 5", and all you fit is a size 0 or 2, you will want to put some weight on or change your workout to build some mass to fit a size 2-4. **I have seen beautiful models go to New York wearing size 0-2 and lose option after option with clients because they are too small to fit the clothes.** Get the weight on in a healthy manner, get up to the right size, and then go forward. What if you photograph too skinny, and go ahead and invest in pictures for a portfolio? You most likely will realize after seeing clients that you are not very marketable and have to gain weight. Then you will have to re-shoot your photographs. That costs money and time. Don't run into a double investment that could have been avoided at the beginning.

You don't want to be overweight. You will have to decide what size you are comfortable with because **there are so many different sizes for women in modeling.** You can be a couture, high-fashion model – which is mainly a size 2-4, sometimes a 4-6 — and fit the designer clothes. You can be a fashion/catalogue model — which is anywhere from a size 4 to 8. The majority of agencies represent models that are couture and catalogue. These two categories book the majority of advertising, designer campaigns, catalogues and editorial but, there is still a demand for other sized models.

Plus-size models can get away with a larger shape, but they have to be toned and in shape. The plus-size consumer doesn't want to look at an advertisement of a plus-size lingerie model who's out of shape. That is not what the consumer is aspiring to be.

You can be a size 10 model. These days, there are more clients asking for size 10 models. In New York City, there are several agencies with specialty divisions focusing on women sizes 10 and up. They wouldn't have the divisions if there wasn't a need for it.

Many times our business is considered the main reason for eating disorders. I do not believe this at all. Eating disorders are caused by not wanting to be educated to what is truly healthy. Today they are coming out with study after study proving that thinner is better and healthier. They are taking mice, lowering their caloric intake by 60%, and the mice are living 50% longer. Of course, we are not mice, but isn't that how most studies for humans begin? Take a look at studies on people over the age of 100 and their average lifetime weights. I think it's enlightening to know that if your young model is slim and practicing healthy eating habits, that he or she may outlive us all.

The U.S.A. as a nation eats too much. It is the heaviest nation in the world. Look at the statistics of the country's health for people fifty and over, and you will see a long list of health problems caused by poor diets and over eating. I highly recommend reading the cover story from *TIME Magazine*, October 20th, 2003, and *National Geographic*, "The High Price of Fat" cover story, August 2004.

I applaud our business for showing models of all different types now. We want our children of all different sizes to grow up with healthy role models. **What is really essential is that we promote healthy habits** – eating right, exercising, drinking water, and getting enough sleep.

Models must look healthy. It is a priority. One of the first things I stress is that models cannot skip meals. It lowers their metabolism as their body goes on emergency reserve to preserve energy. I don't ask models to eat like birds. I ask them to eat healthy foods in correct portions. *National Geographic's,* "The High Price of Fat" has a great 2-page layout showing normal, every day objects for correct portion sizes. Did you know that a portion of cheese is the size of two dominos? Or that a portion of meat is the size of a soap bar? I also recommend that models get the right oils in their bodies for digestion. A healthy oil for cooking is olive oil. *Carlson's Lemon Flavored Cod Liver Oil* does wonders for the body, digestion and skin.

It is painful to watch a young hopeful whose face is perfect for couture fight and fight to get to a size 4 when she just isn't able to do it. I always tell models to just do their best, do it healthy, and we will help them build a career for who they are at the size they are.

I have a fabulous model with red hair. She is so gorgeous and frankly, she doesn't want to be smaller than a size 6. Yes, as a good agent, I have to remind her that if she was a bit slimmer, she could book the big editorials and couture campaigns. But then, I always chime in that she should be happy first, and that I am more than happy to promote her at the size she is. I **think it's important that you be who you are, and find an agent who likes you for who you are – face, size and all. At** the same time, be realistic that you may not be the right size for certain agencies and clients.

In regards to bust size, it will depend on your overall clothing size. Most typical fashion models are either an A-cup or B-cup. Some models are B/C-cup. The straight B-cup works the most because they fit both lingerie and swimwear as well as couture clothes. A-cups fit couture, slim-lined clothes better. B/C-cups fit lingerie and swimwear better. If you are a plus-size model, you will be able to have larger breasts since you are allowed a more generous hip size because they complement each other. For fashion/couture models wanting to work in Asia, a C-cup is too large because women in Asia don't tend to be large breasted.

I feel unbiased about breast enlargement. It should never be a judgment call for the business solely. What if you get in an accident the day after your breast operation and are left with permanent scars on your face that stop your modeling career, but you are left with breast implants that you never wanted for your personal self in the first place?

Make sure that if you choose to have breast implants, that you do it because it makes you feel better about yourself. Make sure you are aware of all the health risks and factors involved. Do not get them larger than a full B-cup and make sure they fit your body frame. And without a doubt, make sure you go to a highly recommended top surgeon and check out all of the surgeon's credentials, including licensing and a background check with the National Board of Plastic Surgery.

FOR MEN

You can be slim or muscular. Just don't overdo either. For both couture and fashion/catalogue markets, the general suit sizes are 40 to 42, regular or long. Top-end couture clients tend to prefer suit size 40, but they don't always rule out 38s, 41s or 42s. It varies per market. Whatever suit size you are, agents and clients want models to have nice muscles in the arms but not where it takes away from the line of a shirt or suit jacket. **In other words, don't be bulky.**

It's all about the geometric line of pictures. If you are too boxy in the arms, shoulders and chest, the clothing will look like a box. A box is not the geometric line the clients want. Consumers want to envision themselves being slim and healthy in an outfit, not boxy and bulky.

If a potential male model is weight lifting intensely, I ask him to immediately one down his workout routine on his arms, shoulders, neck and chest in order for him to model couture fashion. The transformation from bulky to modely usually takes 3-6 months.

If a guy is absolutely gorgeous but too skinny, I will wait until he at least fits a 38 suit well and a 40 suit doesn't hang on him. Keep in mind that most fashion clients need you to be a 40 or 42 suit. There are exceptions -- there are enough international markets that are fine with a 38 suit. I have seen male models who are skinny with no muscle definition start their careers out well on the editorial side but, I feel this is a short-term career choice. There are simply not enough clients and

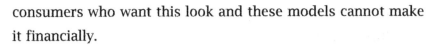

consumers who want this look and these models cannot make it financially.

You want to work towards having good muscle definition. **Agents and clients want male models to be toned, sexy and healthy. It is key to the products men buy which are overwhelmingly geared around power, sex and recreation.** The model has to enhance the product to appear that way to the consumer, who insists on models emanating these attributes.

Overall, men's chests should be nicely defined, but not over board and **stay away from body-builder pectorals.** In regards to stomach muscles, I can't name an agent or client who doesn't love a washboard stomach. **Men should also be cautious about their legs getting too muscular.** If you have an overwhelmingly large thigh muscle, pants will be too tight and not fit smoothly. Clothing is all about the geometric line.

BODY HAIR

For men, it will depend on how much and how dark. **If you have chest hair, most agents will tell you to get rid of it.** Definitely get rid of any hair on your back. Many top models who have a lot of body hair that is long and dark, and/or coarse and curly, will have it removed from their arms, armpits, chest, stomach and legs. The two key areas where it has to go are your front torso (chest and stomach) and the back. I have seen male models with some armpit hair, but the hair is either light colored and minimal, or trimmed very short. You may not need to do anything about your body hair until you gain representation. Then, it can be discussed with your agent.

I recommend laser treatments (see previous Facial Hair section). I think for men especially, it is very hard to maintain the upkeep required for waxing or shaving body parts, such as the chest or back.

For women, you must be well shaven at all times under the arms, the legs and the bikini area. Some models have their arms hair-free as well. It is especially important to learn to shave well in the bikini area without causing skin irritation. Some models get waxed or lasered in this area for this reason. Many models report to me that if they have been lasered just once in the bikini area that they don't have as many breakouts after the hair grows back.

Please, make sure to not get waxed right before a booking. It is best to try waxing at the beginning of your career, not right before you are booked for a job. You never know how the waxing will turn out. If you have reactions, such as swelling, hives or burnt skin, it could cancel you from the booking. I recommend laser treatments to save time and to avoid the breakouts accompanied with shaving or waxing.

Hands

Women should not have long and fake fingernails. Agents and the majority of clients hate them. We prefer that you have well-manicured, short nails displayed on well moisturized hands, period. The longest we want to see your nails is one-quarter inch past your finger and do not do funky, wild nail color jobs. **We want your nails in nice, clear or neutral polish.**

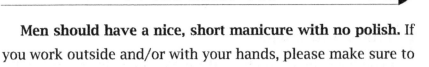
Men should have a nice, short manicure with no polish. If you work outside and/or with your hands, please make sure to remove all calluses. Make sure they are well moisturized and not looking dry, cracked or sore.

FEET

It is important that you take good care of your feet. **Women should have a nice pedicure with clear or neutral polish,** unless requested otherwise by a client. **Men should have polish-free toe nails that are kept well moisturized so the nails do not crack or chip.** Make sure to use a pumice stone on all calluses and hard, dry areas. There is nothing worse than seeing a beautiful model on a beach curled up with horrible looking feet in a picture. Yes, your feet will show up in shots, so take care of them!

In regards to shoe size, your feet are fine unless you wear larger than a Women's size 10 or a Men's size 13. If you do, you will need to make a good investment in shoes of all different types so that you don't lose bookings. No matter what shoe size you wear, you will need to go over this with your agent, as each market varies in regards to the shoes required for bookings. For example, if you are modeling in Kansas City, you will need a good shoe wardrobe no matter what size shoe you are. If you are modeling in Paris, it may not be as much a necessity because most clients bring shoes to the bookings. **Don't forget, if your shoe size is too large, you will need to provide shoes for all markets because the clients may not be able to provide your size.**

TATTOOS AND SCARS

If you have them, you have them. You most likely can't help it if you have certain scars on your body but, it was your choice to have tattoos. **There will be clients that don't mind them, and there will be clients that will.** With scarring, you can try the silicone sheeting or gel noted under "Your Face" section. If they are very serious scars, you may have to speak with a plastic surgeon. With both scarring and tattoos, you will need to learn to cover them up correctly. That means trying out different body make-ups, seeing how well they apply, matching your skin tone, and making sure they don't rub off. It may not be necessary that your scars or tattoos are covered up for all bookings, but it is important that you know how to cover them up just in case.

In regards to thinking about getting a tattoo, I recommend you talk this over with an your agency first. They will be able to give you the pros and cons of your marketability. Tattoos in more hidden areas tend to not be so problematic; however, if you haven't had any tattoos yet, wait and talk it over with an informed agent first.

HEIGHT

Never let anyone stop a dream, but there are height limitations for fashion modeling. **Each market varies and if your height doesn't fall in the realm, it may cause some limitations so be prepared to work harder.** For example, in Denver there is a petite market for 5"4" women for shows. In New York City, petite fashion models are usually more around 5'7". In Japan, females have to be less than 5'10" to do catalogue, but they also prefer them to be at least 5'7". For men, Asia prefers them to be 5'11 to 6'2". In Spain, they prefer men to be 6'1" to 6'2". Still, in parts of Asia and Europe, I have seen women model from 5'6" to 6'0". There are always exceptions for every market. You don't have to set limitations for yourself. **The key is to be aware of what the norms are.**

Overall, average heights that work for most markets are pretty consistent. For women, fashion models usually are 5'8" to 5'11". For men, fashion models are usually 5'11" to 6'2". Of course, there are exceptions, especially when your height is close to the average. I have represented very successful female models as short as 5'6" and as tall as 6'3". I have had successful men be as short as 5'10" and as tall as 6'4". Each market varies, and if your height doesn't fall in the realm, you need to be aware of the limitations.

CONGRATULATIONS!

That is, if you have paid attention up to now and applied this advice to yourself. You have covered the essential top layers in the business. Once you have them down pat, let's get on to what agents call "the must" for every top model.

The **Inner You**

PERSONALITY IS *KEY* IN OUR BUSINESS

All models look great. Accept that point. Being a fashion model is about being beautiful. It's not like you have ever heard someone speak about a model and you visualize an ugly person. To become a model, you have to be beautiful. So, how do you differentiate yourself from all the other thousands of beautiful people in this business?

Many of you are saying, "I have a personality." But the question here is do you have a personality that works for our business? Unfortunately, but true, many international agents have a problem with Americans. Reason being, they feel that models from other markets work harder, are more expressive and are nicer. They think it is difficult to get across to Americans that the business is just not waiting for them to come on the scene. There are thousands of young people entering modeling from all over the world. We are very lucky in North America and sometimes we take it, and people, for granted. It's crucial you are professional, expressive, uninhibited, outgoing, super nice and realize that the competition is fierce.

For teens, super agent Guido Toured says it best: "The key is personality. Teens are in a natural changing process of transition becoming adults. I think that this process cannot be changed or forced into making them someone else. It has to be a process of self-realization, helped with constructive and inspiring suggestions from agents and parents. The key issue concerning those personalities who are still 'green' and growing, is not to make them feel there's something wrong about them. More life experience is required through friends, trips, cultural activities that let them express their personalities and bodies, but at their own rhythm. Self-awareness, intuition and social creativity will all help them grow into the type of personality that is needed in our business. It's just a matter of time."

You must look at your personality coming forth as a crucial step necessary in the modeling world. It doesn't mean you can't enter modeling while still working on your personality, but it may mean that while you are in the personality building process, that other models with open personalities will be booking jobs before you.

Make your personality the most beautiful asset you have. Only YOU can make it show. No one can make you have a beautiful personality. Only you can pull it out so everyone can see how beautiful you truly are!

Thankfully, there are ways to pull that wonderful personality to the forefront. You know it's in there. You talk to yourself all day long inside your head. **Now, you have to work on making it come out so everyone else can see it as well.**

BE EDUCATED

Get an education, know about the world, be interested in music, art, theater, books, politics, nature, travel, hobbies, sports and other interests. **Speak and write in complete sentences.** If you travel as a model, learn a bit of the country's language. Have a sense of class, whether it is earthy and natural, or sophisticated and high end.

BE POLITE

Being nice and polite to everyone you meet will always make your personality more beautiful. **Never be rude.** There's no point to it, it speaks badly of you, and no matter what the situation is, you are always the better person when you respond with class.

DO NOT BE SHY

This will definitely kill you in the fashion industry. No one wants to work with someone that can't communicate. Being a model is communicating an image, a style and feeling directly to the consumer. Agents want to see an uninhibited personality that says, "I will be this comfortable in front of the camera." **Your shyness tells the client they will have to pull every look and emotion out of you to get the booking done.** You will have to overcome this.

HERE ARE SEVERAL TECHNIQUES YOU CAN TRY:

✦ **Talk to salespeople.** Ask the cashiers at stores how their day is going. Ask how long they have worked there. Talk about the weather. Tell them a bit about your day or tell them a funny story as to why you bought a certain item. The point is to get comfortable with talking to strangers.

This is a great way to make conversation with someone you don't know on a personal basis and in a safe public setting. You will have to start up conversations with clients at castings all the time.

✦ **Learn to take five minutes telling a parent, a companion, or a friend about your day.** Set a timer and make sure you go for a full five minutes. You can do it. You think in your head all day long. You just have to learn how to get some of it out there to us.

✦ **Be an initiator and call more of your friends on the phone.** If you can't think of something to talk about, play twenty questions with them. Beforehand, write up a group of questions to ask them. This is a good way to learn to be interested in others and their lives. Many people have the opinion that models are self-centered and it's all about them ("Enough about me, what do you think about me?"). This is a great exercise to learn to talk more, as well as coming into understanding other people's lives. Clients will love you for caring enough to ask about them.

✦ **No one word answers.** Do not allow yourself to speak in monosyllabic phrases such as "yes," "no," "maybe," "fine," "good," etc. This is a big, big one for young models to overcome. **I will talk to a new model on the phone and all I can get is "yes" and "no".** To start with, learn to repeat the question in the response. "Do you like Paris?" Your response: "Yes, I like Paris very much." So much better than just a "yes". By you speaking more, people will be able to sense more of who you are and that is the whole point.

✦ **Make your body part of your personality.** I bet you probably know someone who talks with their hands while speaking. That is what I mean! Use your body language. It helps your personality shine and definitely makes you expressive in the eyes of clients.

DO NOT BE SELF-CENTERED

This could kill your career. No one wants to work with a person who is completely self-centered and narcissistic. **About half the young people who enter the business were probably thought to be the most beautiful person in their hometown or school.** Because of this, they are used to being the center of attention. Once they enter modeling, it's a big, big lesson, that there are many, and I mean thousands, of people just as beautiful as they are. It doesn't mean you are a bad person if you are self-centered. It could possibly be learned behavior from your environment but, in the fashion industry, it is one characteristic you will need to lose immediately. Once you meet some models from Brazil, you will see that they know how to work the agents and clients, and it has nothing to do with them being self-centered. It has to do with them being smart and sweet. Brazilians know how to schmooze and make people feel good perhaps better than any other models I have ever met. Learn to put the focus on others first.

✦ **Make sure to listen.** When speaking to friends on the phone, listen to them first. If you have to speak first, start by asking questions about what they have been up lately. Keep asking them more and more about the subjects they are speaking about. Make others feels good about themselves. **Make it clear that you are listening, genuinely interested in what they have to say, and you are happy for them.**

+ **Turn conversations away from you.** When a friend calls wanting to know about your day, turn it around and say, "Let's talk about you first." The key here is to not interject and veer the conversation back around to you.

+ **Go an hour without being the focal point.** If you are out with friends, go an hour without interrupting, don't make yourself and your opinions seem more important, and learn to listen to others. I am not self-centered but I am a big talker and I have to fight myself to work on this point a lot. It's a very good exercise, and it opens you to other insights and opinions that you might have otherwise missed.

+ **Don't think just about you. If there is a problem that arises,** stop thinking about how it affects only you. Try to see the other person's involvement and how it affects them. This is a biggie. **I have seen models involved in a booking crisis, and all they care about is what they are getting out of it and nothing else;** therefore, the problem can't be solved to help everyone. If only one party wins, no one wins. Most problems are best resolved by all parties being equally and fairly supported.

DO NOT TALK EXCESSIVELY

I could go on and on about this. Why? Because I am a talker. My husband, James, does an imitation of me where he flaps his mouth and then acts as if he is coming up for air and then continues to flap his mouth. If I didn't learn to shut up or have friends that make me shut up, I would kill all my relationships. Thankfully, this wonderful business forces me to listen. I love listening to the agents, the models and their families, and all their needs and stories. It makes me a better person to be there, to listen and to help. **No one wants to work with someone who talks all the time.**

REMEMBER

You are there to model. Yes, they want to know you can talk, take direction and have a brain, but they also want you to be aware that they hired you to get the job done and not interrupt it. It's a bit confusing when our business demands you to have a wonderful personality and be conversational and, in the same breath, demands that you not speak too much so the job can get done. The key is finding the appropriate times to speak and creating balance.

LEARN TO FOLLOW THESE POINTS

+ **Know when to be quiet.** Don't speak to anyone when the photographer is trying to talk to the client or give direction to another model on set, especially if the work area is tiny.

+ **Do not talk about completely inappropriate subjects.** This includes extensive, personal conversations about your private affairs, any prior or present abuse in your life (elaborating on sex and drugs), bad mouthing other clients, agents or models, and discussing viewpoints that might be considered narrow minded.

+ **Let a client know you are polite,** professional, can banter lightly and can show your personality through your modeling, not by talking all the time at the job. By talking all the time or speaking about subjects that go beyond the boundaries of prudence, you are saying that you are more important than the job, possibly inappropriate and insecure. All these can hurt you indefinitely with a client.

YOUR SUCCESS WILL BE MOLDED BY YOUR BEHAVIOR

How you treat yourself and others will reflect how far you make it in this business. You could make it rather far in the fashion industry with bad behavior but, after awhile, it will affect your career in a negative way and your amount of bookings will decline. **No one wants to deal with bad behavior, especially agencies and clients. It hurts everyone when someone doesn't know how to behave correctly.**

A positive attitude goes a long way in our business. No one likes dealing with a whiny, negative person. Look at the bright side of things and be upbeat and optimistic. Agents and clients will appreciate it and it will reflect back positively on you.

Sometimes models find this hard because they see so much attitude and airs thrown around in our business. Having an attitude is just downright insecure, and it doesn't work for long unless you own the magazine or design firm. Even then, it can backfire on you. Don't be intimidated by these types -- keep your attitude in check. **Remember that you always get more with sugar than vinegar.**

DO NOT HAVE PHOBIAS, ADDICTIONS OR BE EXCESSIVE

If you are afraid of large groups of people, if you drink too much, if you are afraid of germs, if you take drugs, if you are promiscuous or any other excessive behavior, this is not the business for you.

If you are phobic, especially about people or germs, there is no way that you can make it through this business. You will constantly be in contact with new places, large groups of people, and many people you have never met before. You will have no way of knowing, nor should you ever ask, about anyone else's hygiene or if they have come in contact with illnesses, etc.

You will have to get your phobic behavior in control or eradicate it. I have represented models who have a deep fear of flying. They realized they had to find ways to deal with it or come to terms that their careers would have major limitations. Models who are very successful have to fly all over to wherever they are booked or where the economy is strongest at the moment.

If you are a partier, it is important that you work on this problem and clear it up. **Even if it is a problem you have overcome in the past, it is very important that you tell your agent.** This way your agent can work with you to avoid this situation ever becoming a problem for you again. If you are a parent, and you know your young adult has had problems in the past, you do not help your teenager at all by avoiding telling us and thinking that your child is starting fresh with a "clean slate". I cannot even count how many times parents have been the culprits in not informing agents of their teenagers' past addiction problems. They allow their young teenagers into an industry where they are asked to make adult decisions and may not be prepared to do so.

Our business resides within the entertainment industry. **It is a business that a lot of people want access to and few are allowed entry. It brings in great people with wonderfully creative minds and so much to give. It also brings in those few undesirables that inevitably want to try to hang in the world of "the beautiful people".** Some of these people will use unscrupulous ways, such as offering free drinks and illegal drugs, to gain entry into the fashion world.

Of course, anyone can run into these problems in any business or any university. Am I to believe that fraternity keggers are proponents of good values and morality? Perhaps, due to the media hype that goes along with the fashion industry, the party scene just seems a little more intensified.

It's important to know your Achilles' heal. You may be too young to know if you could develop a drinking or drug problem but, you should already know if you are the type to take extreme risks or try anything. If you are, **you need to know that drugs and drinking can potentially kill your career and you.** Drinking and drug problems show up in your personality and wreak havoc with your physical appearance. Those responses alone will hurt your modeling career and no one wants to deal with a person having problems with drugs and drinking in any business. The lesson here is to make sure you are strong enough to say "No!" and never let the problem surface at all.

Communication is essential, especially when dealing with problems from your past. I once had a mother who didn't tell me that her daughter had an eating disorder when she was a very young teenager. When her daughter started modeling, the mother went on about how her daughter wanted to be a couture supermodel. Couture models are very slim. I let her know that at her daughter's size of 6 it would be difficult to attain and that perhaps she should try to healthily slim down to a size 4. She did get down to a size 4 and eventually went to work in Paris. After a period of time, her eating disorder became evident. Her Paris agency said she was so painfully thin, looked sick and was missing appointments from being so tired. When I called her mother, I was horrified to find out about her medical history. She eventually had to leave the business. It was so sad. I might not have been able to stop her from going through this problem again but I could have tried, and I wasn't even given the opportunity. The mother felt horrible as well and if she had only told me, it could have all been handled differently.

Communicate with your agent, even if you think the problem is over. Any problems should be discussed -- eating disorders, obsessed ex-boyfriends/girlfriends, abusive family members, medical conditions, learning disorders, etc. **They all need to come out into the open in order for your agency to do the best job for you.**

The vast majority of models lead balanced, clean and healthy lives on all levels. As with all businesses, the media preys on stories that make headlines. Well balanced models don't make great headlines but models in rehab clinics and hospitals do. I want to reinforce this subject because no one wants to watch a beautiful, young person fall prey to any weakness due to lack of information.

The fashion world is based in big cities. It's a vast difference if you come from a small town. Any potential problems can easily be avoided in a small town because certain things may not be available; whereas, you cannot go into the fashion business without the knowledge that you will be working in cities where all forms of positives and negatives multiply. Cities do have fabulous, interesting people, museums, art galleries and theaters, but they also can be a mecca for the bizarre and unusual as well as being more stressful to just function every day. It's just the nature of a city.

OVERALL

Appropriate behavior is important in our business. Clients do want to see charm, excitement and a positive attitude. Sometimes, I see a model cross the line and flirt with a client, which is inappropriate behavior. If a model is shy and has a tough time exuding some personality on castings, I will tell them to act as if they are flirting. I say this knowing that they are so shy that it would never come off as flirting.

Be effervescent and charming, but not a flirt. Clients know it is your job to be charming and show your personality. You have to know where to draw the line. If you come off as a flirt, most clients will take you as being unprofessional, disrespectful and putting them in a compromising position. Coming off as a flirt could also put you into a potentially dangerous situation. Most agencies know their clients pretty well but sometimes a client comes in from out of town, and agents can only do so much background checking. **What if an inappropriate client takes you up on your flirting? Always act professionally.** You can be friendly and charming -- just know when enough is enough.

Do not be condescending. Above all else, don't treat clients with an "I know more than you and I am better than you" attitude. Learn to behave with respect, kindness and understanding. It's always the better road to take and you are affirming that this is how you wish others to treat you as well.

Be humble, even if you think you know more. There is so much to learn from others. This doesn't mean you have to take everything you are told to heart. By listening and learning, you gather more information for your business and you move forward smoothly and effectively. In life, everyone has an opinion but what's the harm in just listening to other opinions? I actually learn the most from my models because they get to go to the markets I may never experience in person. **No matter how much you think you know, it's important to listen to your agents.** We have represented many of you and all that cumulative experience adds up to a lot of knowledge. Our job is to share that knowledge with you.

Treat all people well – from a model you view as competition, the photographer, the client, your agent, the stylist, the make-up artist, and even the person ironing or steaming the clothes for a booking. Always be very nice.

This is one of my favorite stories. I represented a model in New York City. She was a great girl with a wonderful, conversational personality. One day she was at a booking for a high end department store and she noticed the girl who was the assistant steaming clothes for the client and said "hello". Eventually, they struck up a conversation about the city, restaurants and art. At the end of the day, the girl thanked my model profusely for being so nice to her. My model was so surprised by her thankfulness. The next day my model was booked with the same client. **As the day continued, my model realized that the other models were treating the girl quite badly, as if she was their personal maid.** At the end of the day, my model thanked the assistant for all her hard work and said she hoped to see her again.

Little did my model know that this assistant was the niece of one of the biggest photographers in the city. She called her famous fashion photographer uncle on the phone and went on and on about how wonderful my model was to her and how awful all the other models were.

Way too many times, I have had clients or other agents call me to discuss a model's rudeness and disrespect. This type of behavior usually gets the model cancelled and the clients or agents swear they will never use the model again. Now, here was a model that I adored but she in no way or terms had her portfolio ready for one of the top fashion magazines. Yet, because of her kindness, the girl's famous uncle photographer called the agency and requested to see her on a casting. **When she came to the casting, he thanked her for her kindness to his niece and then booked her for one of the biggest fashion magazines in the world!**

That booking changed the entire course of my model's career. To me, that is the essential story on treating all people well. You cannot always tell who is who, who is related to who, who dates who, etc. It's smart to be nice, it's a lot easier on the heart, and it always pays off.

Don't gossip. Our business is filled with gossip and innuendo. You should never gossip no matter what business you are in. It is a dumb career move because it can always backfire on you. Plus, it is cruel, judgmental and usually hurtful. It spells out that you are insecure and need to make someone else look bad so you can feel better about yourself. If you are privy to private information, keep it to yourself. You are a far better person for doing so.

You never know "who knows who." Just like the story above about my model speaking to the girl steaming the clothes, you could be gossiping about a person directly to someone that is related to the subject of your gossip, or they could be dating that person, or work with that person, or they could be best friends. You never know a person's connections so, please, keep your mouth shut.

The only time that sharing gossip is acceptable is when a person's values are being compromised or someone's life is

in jeopardy. I once had a photographer tell me something that was definitely compromising a young model. I toiled for about an hour, as I knew my relationship with the photographer would be over if I opened my mouth. I knew that the model was making wrong choices and setting this straight was far more important. I opened my mouth and would do it all over again because as my priority was the model's protection.

Learning not to gossip is so difficult in our business. It's a people business and people will talk about other people. Just work on it, keep your values high and remember to be kind to others. That should help you maintain your level of gossiping to a minimum.

Be open-minded. To be in our business, you have to be open or tolerant of different lifestyle choices. For example, you can't be homophobic and work in the fashion industry. I personally can't name a major magazine or major agency in New York City, London, Paris, or Milan without at least one gay employee. Also, do not decide that everyone is gay. Quite often friends of mine that are not in the business assume that all male models are gay. I really don't know why they think this other than perhaps they think that fashion itself is a feminine field. Let me set the record straight: The majority of male models I have represented have not been gay.

Veer away from judgement, especially if it is only because they are not the choices you would make. I see models and agents make this mistake and I sometimes make this mistake. **Be who you are but it doesn't mean you have to scream that who you are is who everyone else should be.** Judgement is usually just another form of wanting to control a situation to make things the way you wish them to be. That is just not possible in the fashion business.

If you run in the conservative vein, please keep in mind most agents and clients have city lifestyles that are a bit more off the beaten track than the average person's. They can run artsy with an underground scene attitude and wear all black clothes. Some of them are from old money or entertainment families and have never lived the life of a typical family upbringing. **There is a strong chance that the agents and clients you will meet will come from far different backgrounds than yours.** Remain open-minded.

Be respectful of all religious beliefs. You can be whatever religion you want to be in this business. The key is not to shove it down someone else's throat at a job, casting or in the agency. **Please, don't try to convert someone or to cut down someone else's religious choice just because it is different from your own.** The fashion business is filled with people from all over the world and the world is filled with many different religious beliefs.

Do not be high maintenance. "High maintenance" is a well known phrase in our business. Agents and clients hate high maintenance models. **It means you demand way too much from people, your life is a soap opera constantly needing fixing, and your expectations of this business and people are completely out of sync with reality.** In other words, you take a lot of work and energy. Make sure to be professional, not demand too much, maintain a balanced disposition, and keep a realistic and optimistic approach about the fashion industry.

You are one taking care of one, and that one is you. An agent is one handling many. If you take too much of that agent's time and are not producing the money for the agency to warrant that time, what do you think will happen to you? Most likely, the agency will stop representing you.

I know remaining low maintenance can sometimes be difficult, especially when all you are trying to do is maximize your business. Learn to work with your agency and help them instead of working against them and becoming a nuisance. **It's a business and it takes time. If you want your business to have a solid base, it can't happen overnight.** If by chance your modeling career does take off quickly, a down swing or a lull will usually follow. It is better to be realistic, patient and follow the steps which do take time but can lead to a rewarding career if done correctly.

Don't overstep the boundaries of people helping you. Just because your agent is essentially your promoter and secretary for your career does not mean they are responsible for every step you make. You can make your own plane reservation if the agency asks you to and you don't have to throw back an attitude that you don't do that type of stuff. If they are asking you to do it, they have a reason and, please, if you ever become super successful, don't ask your agent to take care of your laundry or other personal duties even if it means your agent just calls a messenger service to do it. That is just ridiculous. If you are making that kind of money, hire a personal assistant.

Agents don't make enough to warrant that kind of treatment. Treat people with respect.

Be careful of your reputation. Maintain a professional and value-driven reputation. Have integrity. If you party too much, it gets around and it shows on you physically. If you are sleeping around with people in the business, it will get around quicker than a flash and it can jeopardize your career, especially if you accidentally sleep with a client's boyfriend or girlfriend. I have represented a few promiscuous models in my day, and it usually hurts them personally more than professionally at some point. In addition, you are putting your health at risk.

Don't steal or lie. Both can cause your career to come to a screeching halt. No one wants to be around a kleptomaniac. It makes everyone uncomfortable from the model's roommates to the clients. I have seen agencies and clients drop top models over this. Lying doesn't work well either. At some point, it backfires on you.

The age question leads to quite a bit of dishonesty in the modeling industry. The question is "how old are you?" If models are too young for the business, sometimes agents raise their age. If models are starting to get older and feel it will hurt them in this youth-oriented business, they will shave a few years off. I have done both when I was a younger agent. It doesn't make me feel good and I prefer not to now. It is up to each model and how they want to run their business. I think it is much better to tell the truth.

Be laid back and cool. You will hear agents use those words to express what a model's personality is like. It works. These words don't say "shy" or "mean" or "uptight" or "dumb" or "weird" or "high maintenance". They say this person has it together, isn't overwhelming and is someone you want to work with. "Laid back" does not mean they don't express themselves. Successful, laid back models know expression is the key in our business - expressive, just not overbearing. There is a difference.

PERSONALITY CONCLUSION

The perfect model personality falls somewhere in this realm. It is light, positive, charming, fresh, sexy, confident, uninhibited, expressive, happy, loving, caring, empathetic, professional, timely, outgoing, non-judgmental, open-minded, and has values and integrity. Don't forget laid back and cool and always remember to smile from your heart. That alone, can open doors for you that you never knew could open.

Chapter 6

Your **Life**

This is the toughest part of the assessment. Some people want to be a supermodel so badly that they can't look at the realities of what their life is really like.

Here are some scenarios that could slow down the process of your modeling career:

A: YOU ARE YOUNG AND LOOK YOUNG

This is a frustrating point for young teens getting into the business and it is just as frustrating for the parents.

We start models young for the same reasons you are schooled way before college. We want the models to get experience even if it isn't as intensified as their full-time career will be later. This experience also helps models decide if they want to choose modeling as a career because it prepares them for what is ahead.

TRY THIS STATISTICAL DIAGRAM

Draw a triangle on a piece of paper. Most modeling careers begin at the broad bottom of the triangle, which represents all models ages sixteen and under. It's a large group because there are so many young teens who want to model. As you get older you move up the triangle, and models start to drop out of the business. Some make it more of a hobby or part-time job while focusing on their education or a different career. Some decide the business is not for them. Some are not willing to meet the requirements of the business. Some choose to get married and have children, and so on and so forth. Many realize it's just not as easy as they thought it would be. Being successful in this business takes hard work and perseverance. **As the years go on and you age and move up the triangle, the competition gets less and less.** In regards to numbers, modeling is at its most competitive when you are at the young beginning stages.

Now draw an upside down triangle over this triangle. At the bottom of your diagram is the small tip of the triangle you just drew. That is the amount of work available to teens. It is very small in comparison to the amount of teens trying to model. **As you go up the triangle and move into older age groups, the amount of work opportunities expand.** This makes sense because as you get older, you have more spending power, and the largest amount of work in the fashion industry is geared towards the largest amount of consumers.

LOOK THROUGH CATALOGUES

Pick up any large fashion catalogue. Count the number of pages for children, teens/juniors, and adults. Add up the total number of pages for each group and calculate what percentage each group has of the total pages. Clearly, the buying power is with the adults, usually holding about 65-75% of the entire fashion pages. In comparison, the junior/teen pages are usually anywhere from 5-20% of the total.

Some young models take a big portion of that small percentage because they may be the perfect "junior" look and are in demand for a bulk of the available junior work. For the majority of teens entering the modeling business, this is not the case.

If you are a teenager, it may sound strange to you if someone says, "you do not look like a teenager." In our business, it makes complete sense. You may not look like a smiling and spunky teenager but instead may have a beautiful high fashion face caught in a fifteen-year-old body. **You can be a very young teenager and we know you have huge potential for the business. It's just that potential is in the future more than in the now.** It's a waiting game and agencies still want you to gain any bits of experience you can in the meantime.

Some teenagers look older and can pull off a mature attitude on film. These models may gain work since they are pulling up into an older category and larger buying group. Still, being young can cut your work down just due to availability and how some clients perceive hiring models who are far younger than the age and look required for the shoot.

Teenage models are gaining invaluable experience, even if it's just some tests, some castings, or a couple of bookings a year. **Agents can find this age group frustrating simply because models and parents seem to expect too much too quickly.**

Agents can really hype things up when they are trying to secure someone for their agency. It can overwhelm you and your parents. Let's say every agency in New York City wants to represent you and you are fourteen-years-old and you look fourteen. **All the talk about what a big model you're going to be can make you feel as if your career is going to take off immediately.**

I can understand this hype because I can get very excited about a fourteen-year-old with great potential. I am really excited about the *future* potential of the model. I know the model has the potential to have a great career but it's not going to fully bloom right now. Yes, I want the model to start modeling sooner than later because the model can start gaining experience which will give the model a step up when the time is right. **I am excited and should be but I am also very aware it will take time and patience.**

Unfortunately, most models and parents don't see it this way. They expect all that future potential to happen right then and now. They give the agency two to three years with their fourteen-year-old. Then, when the model is seventeen-years-old and ready to go, they leave the agency. They walk with all of the time, money, energy and education that has been gained through their initial agency and start to succeed at another agency. That is why agents can get frustrated and sometimes fearful of a very young teen. They don't want to put all that time and education into someone and then watch them leave right before their time is ready. So, if you are young, please keep in mind how long it will take and the amount of patience you will need. Be patient with yourself and your agency.

B: YOU LIVE FAR AWAY FROM A BIG CITY

If you don't live in an area where there are modeling jobs available to you, then it is just that more difficult. At some point you will have to move to a city where modeling jobs are more available.

You can't expect direct bookings if you are new. Direct bookings are when agencies can book a model into their market that is not based in the market at that time, or when a client books a model in a market to another location. Direct bookings happen occasionally but they is rare. They are especially rare for a new model if the economy is not going well. Clients don't have the budget to justify flying someone in for a job that hasn't built up a resume of experience.

Agencies will try to get you bookings if you live out of the market but, please keep in mind the amount of models that are in that city and readily available. These models are also available to be seen in person at castings. You are living far away and are not available for castings. **If you are young or for whatever reason cannot move, you will have to accept this as a short-term limitation to your career until you can move.**

C: YOU ARE IN SCHOOL

Like any business, you get out of it what you put into it. If you are available only five days a semester, how can you become a supermodel when you are putting in a total of ten days over two semesters and 60 days in eight weeks in a summer? You can develop during these times you are available and you can definitely gain some great experience. but, **you will have to maintain a reality check about what you and your agent are capable of doing for your career in such a short time.** This is especially true when you have only seventy days available out of three hundred and sixty-five days a year. That is less than a twenty-percent ratio of availability.

Think of the t-shirt shop scenario. **If your parents own a t-shirt shop, and they are open seventy days of the year, how successful will they be?** Can they get enough buyers into the store in those seventy days to make a living? Probably not. Perhaps the supermodel days will have to wait until you are out of school. If you begin modeling at the age of fourteen, this could mean when you graduate at eighteen. Keep it all in perspective. The main point is to garner experience, no matter how small it may seem, and spend this slower period of time to educate yourself as much as possible about the fast moving fashion business.

D: YOU HAVE THE HOME-SCHOOL OPTION

If you have a way of being home-schooled while you model and travel, you will have a lot of freedom to grow in our business. **The industry has a stated reluctance to do this because educated models are the first priority.** I would be lying if I didn't say that I jump for joy inside when I meet a fabulous sixteen-year-old teenager who is or can be home-schooled. Why? Because I know this model is going to have more opportunities at a younger age to develop a portfolio. Plus, this model will get an extra education of a lifetime. This teenager will travel, learn about different cultures and history, and at the same time, will learn to run a company. That company is the model. Home-schooling is still prioritizing education and along with the travel, is like taking additional work for extra credit.

THE HOME-SCHOOLING OPTION CAN WORK IN SEVERAL DIFFERENT WAYS.

Some models live in a market with lots of work opportunities for them and their families choose to home-school because they find that model bookings are too often conflicting with school attendance policies.

One way that home-schooling really is a positive is when young teenagers have opportunities in other markets and can travel full-time with a chaperone. A good chaperone may be a parent, grandparent, cousin, sibling, or even a responsible and trustworthy young adult from your neighborhood. Please keep in mind the additional costs of a chaperone because agencies usually do not cover or advance this expense. **When agencies advance anything from airfare to accommodations to photo shoots, the model has to pay it back, usually in the form of bookings, somewhere down the road.**

Advances are loans. They are the agency's investment in the model's career because the agency believes the investment will come back as profit in the future. Many times when I have a young model that is in demand, parents will state that the agencies should be advancing their expenses as well. An agency offering a model to come to their market does not in any way mean there are no other models for them to make the same offer. Please keep in mind the thousands of young faces out there available to the markets. You or your teenager is not the only one they have been waiting for. You will have to consider this when negotiating with agencies. **Taking a "you're going to have to pay to get me" attitude won't get you very far at all.**

Agencies, depending on the situation, will advance on new faces that are perfect for their markets. They are far more likely to advance on a model with strong experience and a portfolio to match. Think of it as a model going to modeling college. If you are brand new and have no prior experience, why should agencies give you a scholarship? Doesn't it seem much more likely they will give the scholarship to the model who has been to modeling high school? The lesson here with advances is to be careful of what you demand. Make sure you have the real bargaining power to do so.

Home-schooling can also work if teenage models are mature enough to travel on their own. In this case, teenagers have to be mature enough to learn to manage their time and do their homework on their own around their modeling obligations. Make sure to check how the agency supervises underage models for safety. Keep in mind they cannot babysit your teenager. This option only works if you feel comfortable that your teenager will be okay without a full-time chaperone.

Some parents choose to let their teenagers travel alone, especially if they have other children at home and/or work full-time. Generally, most models are not ready to travel alone until they are at least sixteen years of age. Parents should only do this once they have been shown that the agency will take good care of their teenager and if their teenager is very responsible and mature.

I don't have an issue with anyone ages sixteen and up traveling on their own. As a teenager, I was too stuck to home and my parents. My parents had to do something to break the umbilical cord. My parents sent me to France at the age of fifteen for a summer. I had adult supervision and the experience made me grow up a lot. My parents taught me to start being independent instead of co-dependent. Parents will need to make this judgment call. **If your teenager is immature or wild, don't do it.** If your teenager is mature enough, try to go with for the first week, meet with everyone at the agency, look all the agents in the eye and make sure you trust the environment your son or daughter will be in.

E: <u>YOU ARE IN COLLEGE</u>

Going to college full-time could possibly affect your career to some extent, depending on what level of modeling you want to attain. **If you have plans of being the next supermodel, college could potentially put a dent in your plans.** As I have said many times, this business is youth driven. If you plan on attending college immediately following high school, it is impossible to model full-time. Like any other business, to reach the highest levels in modeling it will take all of your available time, and that time has to be free Monday to Friday during normal business hours. This especially holds true if you plan on being a successful model in the top markets, such as New York and Paris.

If your plans for modeling are mainly focused on good catalog markets such as Chicago or Dallas, you can probably somewhat juggle modeling and college. These markets aren't as demanding as the top markets but can still keep you pretty busy during your free time around college. Due to your college schedule, you will most likely still lose castings and bookings around scheduling conflicts.

Markets such as Chicago and Dallas are known as secondary markets. They are geared towards more catalogue and advertising and not so intensely high-fashion usually with less clients. **Since these markets demand more approachable looking models, it may not be as imperative that you have a top notch portfolio filled with editorial from around the world.** Still, when given the chance, clients will work with top models who have strong portfolios filled with editorial. Models that work full-time while you go to college may also have a leg up because they are more available. They may make more money than you due to their years of experience, availability and demand to be booked. **You must think supply and demand. If a model is more in demand, the model's rate goes up to even out the model's availability.**

You can possibly model in the primary markets, such as New York City, and attend college, as long as you are committing yourself to your agency during your free time. I see models that commit themselves to their primary market agencies during the summers and any long breaks they may have from school. This is important. It is very difficult to acquire primary market representation after you graduate from college at the age of twenty-one or twenty-two. The reason for this is simple. By that age, other models have already been working for four years full-time and have extensive model portfolios. It is difficult for you to compete. Plus, you are older, and the agencies are thinking of all the time it will take to develop you. On the other hand, secondary markets are more open to development of older models because there is a lot of work for models in their twenties and early thirties. Make sure to keep your hand in modeling with your free time around your education.

Representation in primary markets can occur after graduation from college. I have done it with some older models. Initially, I would get them experience in markets abroad in order to build up their portfolios. Then, primary markets such as New York City, would be interested since all the base building had been done already and the older model was ready to compete.

For men, the college question is quite different. It can only help your career to model in your teens because you are gaining invaluable experience. Luckily, **the men's market tends to have a broader age range.** Many times I have seen a male model take a year off of college to see if the timing is right to be marketed. If it is not and it has been thoroughly discussed with the agency, they go back to college. **Some men's looks are right for the young, high end editorial and they have to forego college for awhile. Some are not.** There are high end editorial and prestigious designer campaigns for younger and older men. If it is not the right time, they can usually wait until after college and begin building up their portfolio. Then, they still have the option to obtain a very successful career in either primary or secondary markets.

F: MISCELLANEOUS YET IMPORTANT THINGS TO CONSIDER:

YOU HAVE AN UNSUPPORTIVE FAMILY.

If you are underage, this is a problem. You will need your parents' permission to model. Plus, the business can be so difficult and debilitating on your self-esteem that you will want the support of your family. You will definitely need some financial help from your family to get started.

YOU HAVE A STAGE PARENT.

If your parents or anyone else is pushing you into modeling and you do not want to do it, then it will most likely not work. Some parents want their teenagers to model because they wished they had modeled. Some parents want to push their kids into modeling for some ego based reason of proving what their children can do it. **Do not allow your parents to vicariously live their dreams through you if it is not your dream.** Go after your own dream. Never let your music die inside of you.

On the other hand, there is nothing wrong if a parent or girlfriend suggests to you that you should give modeling a try. Perhaps you don't realize how good looking you are. You just have to trust your own instincts to know the difference between a push with intentions that are not in your best interests and a nudge with intentions that are solely looking out for you.

YOU HAVE A SERIOUS RELATIONSHIP, ARE ENGAGED, OR MARRIED.

This is an issue only with traveling. If you plan on being a top notch international model, you can plan on a lot of travel. **Top-level models travel all over the world.** Sometimes they go to markets on stay for two to three months at a time. Many times they are based in larger markets, such as New York City or Paris, and can have bookings on location anywhere in the world.

Sometimes models think they can take their significant other everywhere with them. If you have the money to afford your own hotel and don't mind the fact that you are doubling your expenses, then you can do it. Usually, you cannot. Models' apartments are not made for models and their partner. They are made for models of the same sex. It will cost extra for your partner to go with you and many times your agency will only give you some suggestions for hotels. The rest is up to you because it is really not the agency's responsibility.

Traveling a lot can be very hard on any relationship. Is your relationship going to succeed by your being gone for months and months during the year? This is something that you will need to take into consideration when deciding at what level you want to model. I see models' relationships succeed only when their partner is very secure and has his or her own career and identity.

YOU HAVE CHILDREN.

For the same reasons stated previously, this is difficult. Travel can put a crunch on your responsibilities as a parent. I travel often but it is mainly weekends. I have been divorced and am now remarried. My children are taken care of by family members the entire time I am gone and I work from home when I am not traveling. For us, it works. In general, secondary markets and smaller markets are great for models with families as the travel tends to be far less.

You will have to discuss with your agent how much time you can travel and what is feasible for you and your family. I think that models with children can handle short trips of no more than seven to ten days. Those trips should be spaced pretty far apart instead of back-to-back. Once you get beyond that amount of time, it is too taxing on your children. You chose to be a parent and your children should be your first priority.

YOU HAVE A HAVE A FULL-TIME JOB AND IT'S NOT MODELING.

This is especially difficult if your job is during the day. How are you going to be available for castings? How flexible is your job? Is your job going to let you take off for several appointments a day? How about several appointments a week? And then, if you book one of your castings, are they going to let you take the day off to do a modeling job? How many days a year is your main job going to allow this to happen?

Most models, especially in secondary markets, do supplement their full-time modeling at the beginning of their careers with night jobs. This allows them the flexibility to be available during the day for castings and bookings. They might be a little more tired than the rest of us with only day jobs, but it is the means to the end result. By working at night, they don't have to depend fully on modeling to pay the bills. At the beginning of your career, like any other career, there is the education and development phase with very little or no money coming in. **You cannot count on modeling to pay the bills at the beginning of your career.**

: C h a p t e r 7 :

Reality **Checks**

CASTINGS ARE A BIG PART OF YOUR JOB

You don't get paid to go to castings. You go to castings to meet clients so they can decide if you are right for the booking. Getting the job is the end result where you will finally make money. Don't forget, many other models are hoping to get the same job you are trying to get. Many of them will have more experience and stronger portfolios. Having some other means of making money is important, especially at the beginning.

YOU NEED MONEY TO START YOUR CAREER

It's no different than any other career. It costs money to get an MBA degree. It costs money to learn to be an engineer. It costs money to learn to be a hair stylist. So, why would it be any different if you want to learn to be a model? Agencies will advance on certain things but you will have to be exactly what they want. No matter what, be prepared to invest in your career.

YOU ARE THE PRODUCT

If you don't know the positives and the negatives of your product and you decide to go to market without this knowledge, there is a good chance your product will not fare so well. **Clear out the negatives first.** Then, you, the product, have a much better chance of succeeding.

THERE ARE NO GUARANTEES

There are no guarantees in life. In fashion modeling, there are no guarantees that you will succeed at all. **No one can look at you and "guarantee" you will be a top model. They can tell you that you have all the potential to make it to the top but it really is up to you.**

You could be the top student in your high school class, the valedictorian, with so much promise to be a top doctor. Still, with all of that, no one can guarantee you will succeed. The same holds true for modeling. It takes YOU to take all your amazing assets and utilize them with sheer willpower and perseverance in order to succeed.

YOU MUST BE PATIENT

If this process of self-analyzation takes six months or a year away from you pursuing an agency, it will most likely be worth it. It is worth doing it right from the beginning. Make sure your base is strong and then go forth into business. **The business is youth-oriented and some people get caught up in the fact that they are losing time and aging as they prepare to enter the business.** Time well spent is time saved both financially and emotionally. It is all about quality, not quantity. You will need to bolster yourself up both emotionally and financially so that you are prepared for the fierce competition in fashion modeling. It is better to enter the business a year later and a year wiser than to fail straight from the beginning. You probably have ventured somewhat into our business already. Otherwise, how could you be reading my book? Someone had to recommend it to you. Smart person, you. **It's the best step to educate and prepare yourself first.**

REJECTION HAPPENS EVERY DAY IN OUR BUSINESS

Very few, and I mean very few people make it through one day of our business without rejection. Rejection happens daily. When you are modeling, you go to castings every day or you are on a booking. Most likely, one or more or all of those castings will not book you. There are days when you are not working and your other model friends are working. Usually, that spells rejection to you.

You have to learn to deal with rejection and not take it personally. You have to rationalize the truth that 99% of the time it is not about you as a person. You may not be the exact look they want. A model with more experience may have been booked. It could be a slow time period in the marketplace. **There are numerous reasons that you may not get a job but it doesn't have to be about you as a person.** Being the product is tough because you think, breathe and feel. Your emotions make you take it very personally. Try as hard as you can to not let it get to you. You have to learn to let things slide off of you and move on to the next opportunity.

I find that models take it very personally at the beginning. So do all of us that are new at anything. We are trying to figure out the ropes, hoping we are doing things right and not so sure if we are doing anything right at all. It is a very sensitive situation. **With time, you will learn to roll with the punches and that model booking decisions are truly not all about you.** It is a business choice based on what they need and what products are out there. There are so many great products available to them. Hang in there and know your time will come. Next time, someone else will feel sensitive instead of you.

FOLLOW THROUGH

Hopefully you have taken notes on what you need to work on and what you can reasonably accomplish with your future modeling career. The process itself is a lot to take in. You are being asked to analyze and criticize YOURSELF – not an easy task and not one that most people want to do but, you have to do it. Build your base solid before you start moving up the ladder. Work hard on the points you need to improve. Do not take this book or any agents' advise lightly. **The agents' biggest pet peeve is when potential models do not follow through on advice given.** I can literally think of hundreds of potential hopefuls that never followed through on advice given by me to become a model. **Make sure to follow through.**

From this point on, this book adheres to the fact that you have worked through your self-assessment and are ready to move forward with your modeling career.

Final **Countdown**

DO YOUR SNAPSHOTS

This next step is crucial. I personally feel it is absolutely the most important thing you must learn to do well because **snapshots, or polaroids, are paramount. There is not an agency or client that doesn't ask for them at some point. Many times, final decisions on jobs are based solely on a model's polaroids.** Of course, agencies and clients will look at your portfolio but make-up and hair can do amazing tricks to the eye. They want to make sure you are just as beautiful in your natural form. The only time an agency may not ask for snapshots is because you are there in person, and they'll take some polaroids or snapshots of you while you are there. Bottom line, they have to see how you shoot on film naturally. If you do not master how to shoot snapshots or polaroids of yourself, you may lose great opportunities in the world of modeling.

Snapshots are the best, inexpensive way for an agency to analyze your potential.

You could send in your high school picture or your family pictures to any agency but just to make sure, an agency will ask you to do a basic snapshot procedure. This is their way of analyzing everything that is crucial to our business in one easy step. **Usually your snapshot pictures alone will decide your**

fortune with an agency. Once you are represented by an agency, other national and international agencies will hopefully be interested in you and they will request snapshots as well.

Unfortunately, it's really not an easy thing to learn. **Most people don't know how to shoot their own snapshots correctly.** It's important to work on it now before you enter the modeling business. You will do this procedure over and over throughout your career. The process itself really isn't costly. Use your home camera, buy film at the grocery store, and turn it in at your local store to be processed. You can also use a digital camera and download it on your computer. Just make sure the images are not too high a resolution because they will take too long to e-mail.

THE BASIC SNAPSHOT PROCEDURE

The headings or bold, underlined text will be the general procedure an agency will send to you. It is up to you to use the extra advice to maximize the procedure to make you look your best.

✦ **Get a good home camera.** It doesn't have to be the best on the market but should take a fairly decent picture that isn't all soft and blurry. Some of the disposables are actually quite good. **Make sure your film is 35 mm, 36 exposures** and shoots well inside with natural daylight (don't shoot under fluorescent light) or outside in nice light. I **recommend you shoot several rolls of film.** Use the first roll as a trial run and then use the next roll or two to shoot the best scenario. You can use a high quality digital camera that doesn't make your skin look like a series of dots.

✦ **Pick a well lit location.** Do not take pictures at night. I recommend natural daylight against a white or light-colored wall. I have seen some great photos shot against colored walls but I think it is best to do a trial run to see how you look against this color before shooting and sending it to an agency. You can shoot outside but do not shoot with your eyes in direct sunlight. **Wherever you shoot, make sure the light is not causing any funny shadows on you, your body or the background** and make sure it makes your skin color look good.

✦ **<u>Shoot in a bikini for women and a Speedo or underwear for men.</u>** It is important to get a good swimsuit or underwear that looks good and fits you well. Make sure the color of the garment is working with your skin color and is creating an overall slim, well-toned appearance. **Make sure your swimsuit works for you and not against you.**

KEY AREAS YOU WANT TO MAKE SURE LOOK GOOD:

✦ **The chest** - For women, you don't want to look too flat or too busty but just right for whatever your size is. For men, you want to look defined but not too boxy or too big.

✦ **The waist** - For women, your waist should come in and not be boyish and straight. You can work on this by slightly twisting your hips but keeping your upper torso straight. Just make sure it looks natural, which may take some time to get used to. For men, make sure your waist appears lean.

+ **The hips** – For women and men, hips should be slim. Sometimes men's hips jut out a bit at the top of the hip creating an appearance of a wider mid-section -- which the fashion industry does not want on male models. These models usually have to be a bit slimmer than the norm to create a nice, slim waist and hip line in photographs.

+ **The legs** – For women, they need to be slim, and not flabby. They should not bulge out on the outside or inside too much. For women and men, they need to be toned but not overly muscular.

+ **The arms** – For both women and men, the arms should be toned and in shape -- not flabby and not too overly muscular.

Makeup

<u>**Make sure to wear no make-up.**</u> If you are breaking out, just tell the agency that you are working on your skin and once your skin clears up you will shoot the requested shots. If you have one or two very small blemishes, you can cover them up lightly. **If you shoot with blemishes, most agencies will tell you to work on your skin and then re-shoot the pictures.** So ,why take the pictures in the first place until your skin is clear?

+ **For women, if you want to wear a bit of make-up, make sure it looks like absolutely none.** Do not put on any eyeliner! I have received a lot of snapshot procedures where the model is wearing liner and shadow and I always ask the potential hopeful to re-shoot the snapshots. Do not put on lipstick! **Wear a bit of moisturizer on your lips so they are not dry and cracked. That means chapstick or lotion -- not gloss.**

✦ **For men, make sure your skin has a nice, healthy glow and your lips are not dry or cracked.**

Hair

<u>**Wear your hair naturally and wear it back for half the pictures.**</u> Agents have to see you in the clean canvas form, and that goes for your hair as well. You may love it best stylized,but keep in mind that you are not the artist creating the picture. You are the canvas.

✦ **For women, do not curl your hair or blow it dry into a very set style.** Just let it be. If you have curly hair, it is probably best to do snapshots with it curly and then worn straight because agents and clients may want to see both. If your hair is below your chin or longer, you will need to wear it nicely back in a ponytail for half of the pictures so they can assess your facial bone structure better.

✦ **For men,** wear it naturally for half the pictures and wear it combed back for the other half. **Do not wear gel in your hair.** It makes your hair stick together and the skin on your scalp shows making you look like you are going bald.

Do not wear any jewelry that detracts from your face or hair. Also, be careful how much jewelry you have on the rest of your body. It deters from the clean canvas approach.

Take the following shots

Remember to use the entire roll of film. The agents want to see a lot of film. That is why it is best to shoot two rolls and then send them the very best. You are not a pro at taking these pictures so you might as well give yourself a little bit of leeway and shoot more. **The best way to approach this it to shoot one roll, send it in to be developed and then re-shoot what didn't work.** Just make sure you are wearing the same swimsuit and naturally styled hair both times.

Face shots — straight on and profiles

Face shots are from the top of the chest up. Make sure to do a straight face, meaning no smile, as well as a smile. Profiles should be shot at forty-five and ninety degree angles.

+ **Try lots of different subtle angles** with your face straight on, starting with your head slightly up with your nose a bit up and then slowly half inch by half inch lower your chin until your chin is very low. Then slightly tilt your head to the left and a bit to the right, degree by degree.

+ **Make sure your chin is not doubling** into your neck. Keep it out creating a strong jawline. Some models don't get this. If you were sitting at a table with your elbows propped on a tabletop, and your hands clasped below your chin, that would make your chin stick out right so that there is a definitive jawline. Then release your hands and keep your jaw the same way. Go look in the mirror and you now have a jaw. The key is to make it look natural.

✦ **Try slightly different expressions** – happy, bold, sexy, sly, sweet, haughty – all looks that work for good charisma/attitude on film. The key is to be expressive but to not look sad. Negative expressions don't work well. It is also very important to not squint too much during any of your expressions. Small eyes are not an asset in our business. Also, don't make them so wide-eyed and bushy tailed that you look like a deer stuck in the headlights.

✦ **When doing your profiles,** make sure to keep your chin up enough so that there is no babyfat under your chin, creating a nice long neck. Do not look stiff.

✦ **When doing your smiles,** try everything from the typical graduation picture smile, the sweet child smile, to the sly smile, and the laughing smile. Sometimes smiles work best when you are laughing or smiling off camera a bit. Think of things that really make you smile and laugh.

H IP UP SHOTS — STRAIGHT ON AND PROFILES.

Probably, the most important factor with these shots is that your face and torso looks great.

✦ **For women,** the main problem I see is **making sure there is an indentation at the waist – an hour glass figure**. Some models find that even though they are slim, they may have to be a bit slimmer due to the fact that their waist does not produce an indentation and their waist looks too thick. Again, try to work this by keeping the upper torso straight on with the camera and moving the hips slightly in either direction.

+ **For men,** again, the problem is if they have hips, almost like women do, but boxier. Hips like this do not work in the business. If this is an issue, they usually have to be a bit slimmer than the average male model in order to correct this.

FULL-LENGTH SHOTS - STRAIGHT ON, PROFILES AND BACK

The two key points are for your entire body -- from head to toe -- to be in proportional balance, and that your legs look good.

+ **For women,** your legs should not look heavy on the outside or the inside of your thighs and they cannot be out of shape. Some female models have what agents call "tree legs" which are legs that appear to be the same width from the thigh all the way to the ankles. You want to work on having shapely legs where they are slimmer from the knee down to your ankles.

+ **For men,** you don't want to have bird legs that are too skinny or bulked up, overly muscular legs.

+ **Most models find the full-length back shot unnerving.** It's not always the make or break shot but agents definitely do not want to see a flabby butt, love handles around the waist or any cellulite. Stretch marks and scars can be an issue. You can cover them up and show agents you cover them well for pictures. Body make-up for heavy scars works well for this purpose. When you send in your pictures, **be smart and tell the agency if you have any scars or stretch marks.** We have to know everything to do our best for you. You can jeopardize your agency's reputation and your own by not being up front about issues such as this.

✦ **If you have any tattoos,** make sure to show all of them. Take close-up pictures of each tattoo so that the agency can get a straight forward view of what they are dealing with. **In today's market, you run into a mixed ratio with clients and how they feel about tattoos.** Men with tattoos fare better than women, especially for editorial. Women fare fine if the tattoos are in hidden areas and not straight on the arms or chest. Another good idea is to take a few shots showing that you can cover the tattoo up with make-up.

MAIL YOUR SNAPSHOTS IN WITH ALL YOUR STATISTICS

Make sure to be truthful. There is no point in lying, and it can work against you. **You may be thinking, "If I tell them I am as thin as a fashion model, they will like me." No, that is not how agents see it.** It is very difficult for me when I am looking at snapshots of a model with so much potential but I think the model is a bit overweight. Then, I look at the statistics the model sent me and it states the model is already couture slim in weight. I think to myself, "I'm not asking this model to lose weight or it would be too much." I usually decide not to represent the model because they don't look the right size on film even though it is stated they are the correct weight. So, don't lie. **I would much rather know your real weight and ask you to trim down than just com-**

pletely say "no" because you lied and said you weighed less.

✦ **<u>Height.</u>** This can be tough because if you are female at 5'7. 5", and you know a certain agency only takes models from 5'8" and up, you may feel the tendency to to fudge your height a bit, but what's the point? **Do you want to work with an agency that you can't be honest with?** The agency will most likely put you at 5'8" on your composite anyway. It is not that the agency is trying to lie about your height. The agency is basically grouping you into the closest set height category in our business. If a client or other agent inquires about your real height, your agency will usually tell them the truth. I also recommend going to a doctor and having your height put on an office note. **Heights are disputed often in our business** -- might as well have it from a legitimate source.

✦ **<u>Weight.</u>** This is so important. It is the best way for an agent to tell if a model is falling into the appropriate category for modeling or not. Definitely be honest about this.

✦ **<u>Bust, waist and hip measurements.</u>** If you are unsure of your measurements, you can go to a tuxedo or dress shop and have them measure you. **For women,** you have to know your bra cup size and for your records, it is good to know your measurement right under the bust as well because certain markets request it. **For men,** chest and waist are the requirements.

+ **Collar and sleeve size.** **This is only for men.** Top markets will shy away from collar sizes that are too large or sleeve lengths that are too long because they feel the majority of clients don't make larger sample sizes. **If you run a bit larger in these areas** but your suit size falls in the normal range of a suit 40 or 42, make sure to emphasize this. I represent a male model who is 6'3". His sleeve length is 37 inches which is very long, but he perfectly fits a 40 Long suit. I emphasize this point with agents.

+ **Dress or suit size.** These are perhaps your most crucial sizes. For women, it's okay to state, "I wear anything from a size two to six." They are used to models having this level of flexibility as clothing companies use different gauges to code their sizes. Don't feel you have to be just one size. For men, you have to state the main suit size you wear. You may wear a suit 40 or 41. You can state both but they need to know which one fits you best.

+ **Inseam and outseam.** Most agencies only need to know your inseam which is most easily identified by noting the length of your blue jeans. Just make sure your blue jeans are not too long at the size you prefer to buy. Usually, clients don't want the pants to look baggy at the bottom. **For men, the inseam is crucial** because most men's pants are sized this way. **It's not as crucial for women.** Some Asian markets and some other clients want to know your outseam as well, so keep it for your records.

+ **Shoe size.** There are average ranges of shoe sizes clients will provide at bookings in bigger markets. If your foot runs a little small or big, you may want to put the closest size you fit within the normal range so that clients don't take you off a model list because of it but, you must be able to fit this size if you are at a booking. **Shoe size can be a problem if your foot is larger than a Women's 10 or a Men's 13.** I don't recommend you state only the size within the normal range. For example, if you prefer to wear a women's size 11 but you can wear a tight size 10, you may want to put your shoe size as "10-11". If your foot is bigger, so be it. You will have to acquire a very large shoe wardrobe while modeling.

✦ <u>**Hair and eye color.**</u> If your hair is colored, state what your natural hair color is, as well as the colored version. If you had your hair straightened for the pictures and you are naturally curly, state this as well. Don't forget to note hair extensions or if your hair is chemically relaxed. **Agents have a difficult time gauging a model's full potential if they are not given all the correct and true information.** If you have a basic eye color, state it. If your eyes are somewhat interesting, such as aquamarine or steel blue, feel free to note it to agents.

✦ <u>**Age and date of birth.**</u> Be honest. There is no point in lying. If you are older but know you look younger, state that to the agency as well. **"I am twenty-three years-old but I am constantly told I look as young as sixteen-years-old."** There is nothing wrong with pushing the point in our youth driven business, especially when it is true.

✦ <u>**Ethnic background and nationality.**</u> This always makes a model a little more interesting. Most snapshot procedures do not request it. **I think most agents and clients love knowing what ethnic roots make you who you are.** For example, I am Native American (Creek), French, and Dutch with a wee bit of Irish and Polish. That sounds a bit more interesting than "I am American". Quite often, Asian markets will inquire about ethnic roots. Make sure to state your nationality. Your citizenship is essential when dealing with passports and other international matters.

✦ <u>**Sports and activities you do well.**</u> There are times when clients need models who really can do a certain activity. It is important that you can do it NOW at the level you state to your agent. Please, don't put football if you haven't played on a team in eight years. Think any activity that could get you a booking and note it to the agent. I have models that are top notch at skiing, horseback riding, ballet, skateboarding and swimming, and these activities get them bookings.

✦ <u>**Home address, mailing address, e-mail address, telephone number and cell phone number.**</u> I can't tell you how many times I have received mail requesting me to contact someone back and there is no return address or phone number. **Make sure to include this or how will they ever be able to get a hold of you otherwise?**

SNAPSHOT EXAMPLES

Take a look at the pictures on the following pages to see examples of good snapshots.

Pursuing **Representation**

There are several ways to obtain representation. **I only recommend three ways of getting into the modeling business. They are contacting agencies directly; entering a contest involving a prestigious and reputable client, magazine or agency; or going to a reputable model convention where you have the opportunity to meet many different types of agents in one shot.** No matter what entry you choose, the key is to be professional, outgoing, persevere but do not be a pain in the neck. Presentation is important. It should be professional, informative and not overwhelming.

MAILING YOUR PHOTOS IN

Put a short, nice note with your pictures. It should not be an autobiography. It should simply thank them for taking the time to consider you and write a little bit about yourself. Include **where you are in life,** including **school** and how well you are doing at it, **work** and the hours, and your **family** or relationship. Agencies like to know what **sports** and activities you like to do, what your personality is like, and anything else super interesting about yourself.

Your note should be professional but not as if you work for a corporation. In our business, you are the product. **We don't want your note so cold and formal that we can't see your per-**

sonality shining through. Write professionally but as if you are writing to a friend in business. Keep it personable and outgoing.

Keep it short and to the point. The entire note should be no more than three short paragraphs.

Confirm the address via a short phone call. Your phone call should be nothing but, "May I have your address and zip code, please?" Or, "May I have your e-mail address for submissions, please?" Agencies move as often as people do, and you don't want to go through all this to have your submission sent to a wrong address.

IF YOU ARE PURSUING A CONVENTION

I recommend you check out the convention's reputation first. They will usually have a website and you can see what agencies attend, and you can usually see what level of endorsements they are receiving from agencies and former contestants. This is especially important in regards to what area of the business you are aiming for. **If you are still unsure of the convention's legitimacy and reputation, you should be able to ask for references ,and they will supply them to you.** Make sure to note if you can afford the convention you choose. They range in price from $500 to thousands of dollars. Dependent upon what you can afford, it is a great way to see a lot of agencies in one place.

IF YOU ARE PURSUING A CONTEST

I recommend checking out the contest's reputation. The safest way is to check who is sponsoring the contest. Then, you can investigate the legitimacy of the contest through the clients' own reputation. Contests have very specific dates and rules. Make sure to read through these thoroughly to ensure that you can fulfill each and every obligation and date you must be available, as well as whatever restrictions may apply. For example, most contests have age limits. A good example is a model of mine who entered a major contest via a magazine. She was picked to be a finalist and then couldn't go because school was a conflict. I doubt the editor who called her will forget that in the future. Don't let that happen to you.

IF YOU ARE PURSUING AGENCIES ON YOUR OWN

I recommend mailing to agencies in your immediate area first. If you don't know who is legitimate, you can call the top newspapers, department stores, boutiques and hair salons asking who they would recommend. **You can also buy the *The International Directory of Model & Talent Agencies & Schools* printed by Peter Glenn Publications.** This book is used by practically every agent I know.

IF YOU ARE PURSUING TOP INTERNATIONAL AGENCIES

I again recommend using *The International Directory of Model & Talent Agencies & Schools.* Also, take a look at www.models.com for information on agencies and top models. Unless you're in the know, it's a bit more difficult to know which agencies are legitimate in larger markets.

WHEN MAILING YOUR SNAPSHOTS

Keep an extra copy and definitely keep a hold of the negatives. You can make laser copies if requested to mail them elsewhere or you can print them again.

Include a self-addressed, stamped envelope. This hopefully helps you get a response. Agencies get loads of submissions. **If there isn't a self-addressed, stamped envelope requesting a reply, many agencies throw away the submissions they are not interested in pursuing.** This way, you have a much better chance of getting an answer. Lots of times, "no's" in the form of no reply hang with young hopefuls as a "maybe" or the thought that their submission didn't make it in the mail.

WHEN E-MAILING YOUR SNAPSHOTS

Make sure to note your purpose in your e-mail by stating in **the subject area your name along with "Requested Photos," and if they are unsolicited "New Model Seeking Representation."**

Send them a jpeg file in low resolution (100 dpi is fine) and not too big in size. If you don't know how to do this, go to a computer place that will know how to do this correctly. **You want the download to be easy and fast.** If it takes too long, they will just delete your e-mail because their time is precious. Also, make sure the pictures are not too small or too large. If it's too small, they can't see you. If it's too big, they can't see all of you in the frame of the computer. I have had young hopefuls e-mail me a download of just two pictures and it has taken me over thirty minutes to download. I don't do that anymore. I am nice about it and e-mail back stating, "Your e-mail is taking too long to download. Please try again by sending your download in a much lower resolution and in jpeg file format." You cannot count on everyone to reply like this.

Make sure you can download your e-mail as quickly as possible on your own first. Try sending it to a friend's e-mail to see how long it takes. Make sure to **save your sent e-mail and snapshots on file** in case the agency says they did not receive your snapshots. E-mail is not perfect. Many times my e-mails don't make it to their place of destination. This way you can send the original again and they will know you really did send it in the first place.

FOLLOW-UP

If your shots were requested to begin with, you should request a response. **Follow-up about two weeks after you send your pictures with a phone call checking if they received them.** If you leave a message and don't receive a call back, give it another week and try again.

If you submitted on your own and have received no response within a month, you will have to take that response as a "no". You can send an extra copy with a brightly colored sticky note stating this is your second submission and you wonder if your first submission got lost in the mail. Make sure to have a self-addressed envelope enclosed and let them know you would deeply appreciate a reply. If you sent an e-mail, you can send it again, requesting a response in the subject header.

If you sent an unsolicited e-mail, do not be upset if you don't receive a response. Just like catalogues and advertisements you receive in the mail, they receive hundreds of submissions. **Agencies get so many submissions and many times only reply to the ones they are interested in representing.**

If you receive a "thank you, but we are not interested," do not call the agency to ask why. They get deluged with hundreds of pieces of mail and don't always have the time to explain. You should be thankful they took the time to reply. Plus, due to the large amount of submissions agencies receive, they probably cannot remember which one you are so it's basically a waste of your time.

I e-mail many agents worldwide on models all the time and not all agents respond. I may check once to see if they received it and that's about all I can do. You can hope for a response but you won't get it from all agents. I personally feel that in business it doesn't take that much time to be professional and nice and respond, but not everyone has or makes that time.

OPEN CALLS

Another option to pursue representation is to go to an open call. **An open call is a time frame set aside by a convention or agency for anyone to come in and be reviewed.** It is preferable you get their requirements beforehand, but overall, anyone can come in to be reviewed. I recommend you call and get their requirements along with the address, the general area of town and cross street. Also, get the exact days and times they see models for open call. Make sure to take the phone number with you in case you get lost. Please keep in mind that not everyone in our business has open calls. Some only allow mail-in submissions.

Make sure to be there when open call begins. Most open calls are not by appointment only, so it is possible that a lot of people will show up. Don't arrive too early. Fifteen minutes before open call begins is the maximum amount of time you should allow. The goal is to make sure you get the best opportunity to see the interviewer but don't be annoying as well by being too early.

Wear something that fits your body. They want to see your shape in a classy, natural way and not too revealing. Make sure it fits the form of your body because there is no point in covering things up when they will eventually ask to see you in a swimsuit. I recommend you bring your own swimsuit to the open call in case they ask. Please **make sure that your outfit isn't too outrageous, racy or wild.** I have seen potential models turned down for this reason alone. It's best to be hip, casual and stylish. Don't overdo it -- less accessories, the better. **Make sure your outfit doesn't overwhelm the real product — YOU.** Wear your hair simple, natural and neat.

For women, I recommend a **not too short skirt or fitted jeans, a body-fitting top and a cool pair of shoes, two inches or shorter** preferably. In regards to shoes, make sure they are not too tall or wedge platforms that you think make you look taller. The agency will see these as awkward, and the shoes may make you less graceful. Women should wear no make-up or make it look like they are wearing none. Keep your hair nice and simple, and bring a hair tie in case they ask to see your hair back off your face.

For men, I recommend **nice fitted jeans with a fitted t-shirt or top, and stylish casual shoes.** Keeping it simple is your best bet. Do not wear gel in your hair.

Do not go to open call with acne on your face. That will be an instant deterrent. If you have a few blemishes, you can either let them be or if you don't feel comfortable, cover them up just a bit. Do not put a whole face of make-up on.

When you are interviewed, LISTEN. It is their time to tell you if you are right for them or not. **If you get a "no" don't question the agent to death as to why.** Many times you will get a vague response such as, "You are not right for our agency," "You are too commercial," or "We already have someone that looks like you." With any of these responses, **your questions should be,** "Do you feel I should pursue this with other fashion agencies, and if so, whom?" or "Do you think I should go to commercial print agencies, and if so, whom?" or "Is there anything I could work on that would possibly change your mind or help me get my foot in the door as a model for your agency?"

When your interview is done, you have either gotten a "yes", "no" or "maybe." **Follow through with what you have been told,** thank the agent for his or her time and leave politely.

I have seen people be so rude when they are turned down. There's no point to this. You can't take the business personally and most likely the person that has interviewed you doesn't make the rules for the business for what the clients want or even for the agency itself. Even if you think the agent has an attitude, there really is no reason to lower yourself by throwing it back at an insecure individual. Rise above it and do not react to their bad day. Keep yourself above this type of negative behavior and always be polite. Never burn bridges. If you get other representation, that interviewer could some day change jobs and end up at your agency or become a client. Be smart.

IF YOU GET ONLY "NO" RESPONSES

Getting all "no" responses is tough, especially if you don't get any responses that help you figure out what to do next. It could be your look isn't in now. It could be you don't meet the agencies' requirements. It could be that the agencies aren't looking for new models. It could be anything.

When this happens, I recommend sending out snapshots to commercial/lifestyle agencies. If you really want to model, it shouldn't have to be just about being a fashion model -- it's just about being you. Again, you can check with local newspapers, department stores or other companies that use commercial/lifestyle people for their promotion work and advertising. **All types of looks work in commercial print,** so hopefully this will help you get your foot in the door. Commercial print can be big money, so don't negate it just because you want to do fashion. You can be beautiful, average or just completely zany looking and they might need your look.

Another option is to check into agencies that book models for trade shows. Every major city has trade shows and practically every trade show needs models to promote their products. **The money averages anywhere from $150 - $500 per**

day and up. This can be a good way to get your foot in the door and make some money to help you invest in your career.

By all means, if you get all "no" answers and just love the fashion business, look at other types of careers within the industry. To name a few, you could try to become an agent, a photographer, a make-up artist, an art director or a magazine editor. There are so many options in the fashion industry.

RUNWAY IS A GOOD THING FOR EVERYONE

If you get "yes" or "no" responses, you may want to learn how to do runway. For "yes" models, it is a must if you want to make it to the higher levels of the fashion business. **You really can't become a high end, editorial model if you can't do runway shows for the top designers.**

If you get "no's" and you are the right runway show height (women are usually 5'9" to 5'11", men are usually 6'0" to 6'2"), you might want to try your local department stores and salons for informal or runway work. **Informal work is when you walk into a department store and a model comes up to you wanting to spritz you with perfume, or tell you about the product they are holding, the outfit they are wearing, or show off their new hair cut.** It usually pays pretty well for starters, and again, it helps you get your foot in the door.

Some businesses don't book from agencies while others only book from agencies. Some businesses will do both – hire some on their own and hire some from agencies.

The great thing about good runway experience is that it makes you a better print model. Learning to walk gracefully and emote a feeling to people in person can only help you be better in front of the camera. There is just something about great runway models. They exude a certain attitude. They are also used to maintaining their weight because they must be couture slim for the designer sample sizes.

You can start to learn how to walk for runway rather inexpensively. Watch the television shows that showcase designers, such as *The Fashion Channel* or *E!*. You can record runway shows and then play them back for yourself practicing along with the models on the runway. It's invaluable to learn from top models and it's free.

I think it is difficult for most young women to learn how to walk in high heels or stilettos. I recommend models work on this at home by wearing at least a 3-inch heel or stiletto around the house for as long as possible. Most young women only wear high heels on special occasions so they are not comfortable walking in them for shows. Wearing heels around the house allows models to get comfortable walking in them.. Over time, the heels will become second nature. Then when they are at a show casting, they are ready and have that much more of a chance of getting the job.

If you are really into making your runway walk better, I recommend top runway model, Carla Fisher. She is flown all over North America to speak on modeling and teach potential models how to do runway. You can check out Carla's website at www.carlafisher.com. Carla is full of wonderful advice. If you are able to go see her speak and work with her directly, she is definitely worth it.

ACTING IS A GOOD THING FOR EVERYONE

Whether you get "yes" or "no" responses, you should check out acting, especially if you get "no" responses and your heart is still beating wildly for the entertainment business. Beautiful people like Nicole Kidman and Brad Pitt become international superstars, as well as diverse looking people such as Danny DeVito and Kathy Bates. Either way, you have to have what it takes to act and that means you have to study.

You have to learn your craft to become a great actor. You have to start somewhere. If you are young and living in practically any town, you can try local theater to see how comfortable you are with acting. You will only learn your craft by studying, taking drama classes or on-camera courses, watching great actors on film or in theater, and reading as much as you can on the subject. All of these things really help accelerate your options because you are connecting into the business more, and hopefully doors will open for you.

One note about theater: Most acting coaches and agents feel too much theater training can make a potential film actor too loud and too exaggerated in movement and voice due to how you must "over-act" to come across to a large audience. For theatrical agents, this may be fine. **Film is very subtle and not over-acted.** On film, you can whisper and the audience will emotionally connect with the character. Some top agents and coaches in Hollywood do not want future hopefuls to study too much theater, if at all. They prefer young hopefuls study dance to learn how to "talk" with their body language. Then, when you are ready to act, they recommend you study on camera and film courses.

If you are modeling, acting experience makes you that much of a better model. **Agents live for models that can act.** It makes such a difference. If you're a model but don't want to become an actor, you may still want to get hired for television commercials for fashion. Make sure to take an on-camera class so that you are prepared for these auditions.

Once you are professionally modeling, your agency will either have a television division or should have contacts at acting agencies for you. If you are modeling in a city, there should be some good, experienced acting coaches in the area. You can check with your local theater groups or colleges to find good acting coaches. Make sure the acting coach's credentials include training in film.

If you are investigating a career in acting, **I strongly recommend you read Jon Simmons' book,** *"Hey Ma, I'm Going to Hollywood!"* You can order his book through <u>www.simmonsandscott.com</u>. This hands-on book is great, simple to read and very informative. It goes through the steps of how to get yourself to Hollywood and the first things you are going to encounter in your career. It is not a book on how to act, which should only be handled through an experienced acting teacher, which Jon is as well.

WHEN YOU GET POSITIVE RESPONSES

First thing, **make sure to read the previous headers on "Runway" and "Acting".** Both of these areas can only enhance you and make you a better model.

Getting a positive response is exactly what you want. It doesn't happen to everyone, and it's such a great feeling of validation that all of your hard work up to this point has been worth it. It also makes you feel that what you want to do as a career is possible!

NOW YOU HAVE TO GET REALISTIC.

"Yes" responses don't always mean a definite contract with an agency. It's only the beginning, and you have just chopped a chip off a very huge iceberg. It is a very nice chip to start with.

If you get a positive response, it is your responsibility to follow through. Following through is crucial from this point on. **Here are some scenarios of positive responses.**

"WE LIKE WHAT WE SEE. WOULD YOU PLEASE SEND US MORE FILM?"

Follow through. Send them more pictures but ask them what they want first. They may want you to shoot with a photographer so they can visualize in print how you will work for fashion. Most likely, you will be required to pay for this investment. No matter what, this photo shoot can usually be used in your future model portfolio.

They may just want you to take more snapshots (*see the snapshot procedure*). **When you are requested to do more snapshots, there is something they are not definitely sure about in the previous ones you sent.** Perhaps, you should analyze if you need to be showing more personality and expression, or perhaps you need a different swimsuit, or maybe better light in the shots. You can always ask if there was something in the snapshots you already sent that can be improved upon.

Sometimes agencies request "be yourself at home" snapshots with you lounging around and doing the things you normally do. This is a great way for agencies to see your personality. **Show lots of personality.** Be cool, laid back and hip, or cute and zany, cuddle your dog, hug your mom, hang on the swing set in the backyard, or show them the house. This lets them know who you are as a person, and at the same time, shows off your personality.

Sometimes, agencies will request a home video, especially if they cannot see you in person. Usually, the video consists of a segment that is filmed very much like the snapshot procedure followed by you walking as if on a runway and ending with you talking about yourself giving them a short biography of who you are and what you do. While speaking, include your age, height, measurements, phone number, hobbies, sports, school and work. I recommend a bathing suit for the snapshot procedure part. As for the runway section, I recommend women wear a hip top and a classic skirt with nice high heels , and men should wear a fitted top and jeans along with casual upscale shoes. The entire tape should not be more than three minutes long and make sure to be naturally you.

When agencies request more, let them direct you in what they want. You can always ask what they want. Do not be overbearing , analytical, or taking up too much of their time. Keep your questions short and simple.

"WE LIKE YOUR LOOK. WE NEED TO SEE YOU IN BETTER SHAPE."

This is exactly what it means. **Follow through. You need to get in better shape.** Ask them from your height, weight and measurements where they would like you to be. It may be just toning up. It may mean dropping or gaining some weight. Let them guide you to what they need. Once you are in the shape they want, re-do the snapshot procedure.

If you don't think you can fulfill this request, let them know and thank them for their time. Also, let them know that if you change your mind within a short amount of time, you will get in contact with them once you have completed their request.

"WE LIKE YOUR LOOK. WE NEED TO SEE YOUR SKIN IN BETTER SHAPE."

Depending on your age, this can mean several things. **If you are younger,** it can mean you have typical teenage acne and will need to clear it up. **If you are older,** they may want you to work on making your skin look healthier and younger. If you are too tan, you will need to lose the tan so they can get a better idea of the condition of your skin. If you have scarring, you may need to get rid of them. Ask the agency to be specific about what they mean exactly and then go back to the section about facial issues under "The Outer You".

"WE LIKE YOUR LOOK BUT YOU ARE TOO YOUNG FOR US. PLEASE KEEP US UPDATED."

This happens quite often to young girls, ages eleven to fourteen. It essentially means you will have to wait. The agencies are showing interest. They just want you to get older, and then you can update them with snapshots again so they can see if you are still what they want. Usually, this request is made if they wish your height was a little bit taller or that some of your baby fat would fall off naturally. **You can't grow up any quicker so you must know the response is positive and have patience.** Sometimes, agencies have to respond this way as they have age limits.

THERE ARE SEVERAL REASONS THAT AGENCIES HAVE AGE LIMITS

You change dramatically due to hormones in your young teens. **For example, if you are a female at the age of twelve,** you could be perfect model shape. Then, your hormones kick in within the next few years and you could blossom to a C-cup bra size with 37-inch hips. If the agency that is interested in you is strictly an editorial couture agency, you would most likely have grown out of their requirements. **If you are a male at the age of fourteen,** you could look perfect as well. Then, in the next few years you could really start to shoot up in height and you could become 6'4". If you had sent your snapshots into a strictly high-fashion agency, most likely you would now be too tall for their agency requirements. **Due to the growth spurts that occur in young teens, agencies are conservative about who they take on at such a young age and prefer to be updated with your development until you are past your main growing years** and then a final decision on representation can be made.

Certain markets do not have much work for young teenagers. Agencies in certain markets don't want to sign on a model, do the development work, and then have the model get frustrated with his or her lack of career progress due to lack of work available in the marketplace.

Some agencies prefer to work with models that are mature and have made it through the essentials of their school education and social development before going into a career that demands they act professionally.

"WE LIKE YOUR LOOK. IF YOU EVER MOVE TO OUR MARKET, PLEASE COME INTO SEE US."

Some markets are just not interested in models unless they live close by. If you get this response, **please do not fly out to the market to see the agency.** They are simply stating the truth. They are not the type of market that books models from outside of their area. If they really want you to move to their market immediately, they will ask for snapshots, discuss it with you on the phone and try to convince you to make a decision to move to their market.

"WE LIKE YOUR LOOK. IF YOU ARE EVER VISITING OUR MARKET, PLEASE COME IN TO SEE US."

Again, please don't buy the next available plane ticket and fly out to their market. This response usually occurs when they kind of like something about you but aren't absolutely sure. **Some people get this response and think they must immediately invest in getting there.** It's truly a pretty lackadaisical response and means exactly what it says: "IF you are here, you are welcome to come on by."

If you get this response, don't be downtrodden because I have seen had many models convince me in person. Only go to the market when you are really visiting there or are checking out other agency options. Of course, a reason for you might be that you really want to be a fashion model. Just remember, there are no guarantees.

FOLLOW THROUGH ON REQUESTS

Make sure to follow through on their requests. **Once you have accomplished the requests, follow these guidelines:**

+ **Don't call** unless they have requested a call or to see you in person.

+ **If it has been awhile** since they contacted you with their requests, do call to make sure your contact person is still at the agency.

+ **Do the snapshot procedure again** to show you have followed through on their requests. Make sure to include a short thank you note noting they requested these changes along with your name, height, measurements, age, phone number, home and e-mail addresses.

✦ **Mail in the requested materials immediately.** If you want to make sure they receive your package, send it express or priority with signature confirmation. This way, when you check with the agency and they say they haven't received your materials, you can check with the express courier company for a signature. Once you know the agency has your materials, **please give the agents three weeks to review everything.** If you haven't heard from them by then, go ahead and politely inquire with your agency contact.

Hopefully after completing the requests, you should get an answer. If by chance it is negative, please go back to the "no" section for further advice. Otherwise, if you received a "yes" congratulate yourself and move forward to the next section!

The **Ultimate "Yes"**

The ultimate "yes" is when you get a call or letter and they make it clear that you have a great look, are perfect for them, and they would love to represent you. If you live close by, they would like to meet you in person to discuss everything as well as go over the contract. If you live further away, they will try to discuss their plans for you via phone or e-mail and will ask you to make a trip to their market. As with anything, you still run the risk of a "yes" turning into a "no", but things are definitely looking good!

PREPARING FOR A "YES" MEETING

The initial meeting can be crucial. You need to have certain things answered and the agency needs to feel a certain response as well. If you are lucky enough to have more than one agency interested, this meeting is paramount to your decision making.

First decide if every question you have running through your mind has to be answered immediately. For example, **I will have a mom ask me, "Where do you see my daughter in five years?" That is an extremely nebulous question and it absolutely does not need to be answered during an initial meeting.** How could I possibly have a clue where a model's career will be in five years? So much of it depends on the model's evolvement and anything can change — the business, the trends, the model's own choices — and I would basically be guessing. If you ask this question, you really aren't getting any concrete information in return because it's not a practical question.

Before the meeting, write down all of your questions. Ask yourself, "Does this need to be answered in this meeting now or can it wait?" or "Can someone else answer this for me?" Delete the questions that do not need to be answered immediately. Keep your questions to the precise things you need answered at the beginning.

GOOD QUESTIONS FOR A "YES" MEETING.

+ What is your agency's reputation?

+ What type of models do you represent? Can I please see some of their composite cards and portfolios? Can I please have your website information?

+ How available do I need to be for castings and for bookings?

+ **Can I go to school and model?** Can I have another job and model?

+ What will be involved in my development?

+ **What will be my initial investment?** Photo shoots? Classes for runway or commercial work?

+ What investment does the agency make in my career?

✦ Is there anything about my appearance that will have to change in order to model for your agency?

✦ **How long is your contract? Is it exclusive?** What if the agency or I want to break the contract? Will I be able to show this contract to a lawyer? When do you expect the contract back?

✦ What type of work will I be doing for your agency?

✦ How much notice will I get for castings and bookings?

✦ **How long do you think it will take for me to start working?**

✦ How do bookings work?

✦ Do I have to do all the bookings you call to confirm?

✦ Do I have a say in what type of bookings I am submitted for?

✦ **What are typical rates and hours for bookings?**

✦ **How and when am I paid after a job? How much commission do you take from my paycheck? How are taxes handled?**

✦ Do you have a TV/film division or will I have to secure another agency for this?

✦ Can I direct book from another market into your market?

✦ **For my look, how much work is in your market?** I know it is just an estimate, but if I do all the right things, how much could I possibly work in your market?

✦ **Will I need to travel to other markets** to build my portfolio in order to make this a sustainable market for me?

GOOD QUESTIONS FOR PARENTS OF AN UNDERAGE MODEL

✦ How do you work with minors in the business?

✦ **Is it legal for underage models to work in your market** anytime during the day?

✦ If I am not available to be with my underage child, **who will supervise?**

✦ **How much work is there for teenagers in your market?**

✦ How often does my teenager have to be available? Am I allowed on castings and bookings? **How do you work castings and jobs with school?**

✦ **Will I have a say on what clothes are being modeled?** For example, if we are at a job and I think something is too revealing for my young teen?

✦ Since my teen will be changing a lot in the next couple of years, **how can we be careful to minimize the investment so the cost is offset by work?**

✦ How old will my teenager most likely be when modeling could become a full-time responsibility?

A special note to parents: Be involved in the meeting but don't take it over. Teach your child to run his or her own company. Be the CEO and make your young hopeful president. Make them ask questions and get answers. You can insert your thoughts when necessary. Models who are co-dependent do not fare well in our business. Make your young teen independent and business savvy.

It is very important that you maintain a positive attitude. Be sweet and be wonderful. The agency is assessing during this entire meeting if they want to work with you. No one gets anywhere by being negative or having an attitude. Yes, this is a serious meeting, but if you come off too serious, the agency may not want you. Agents want to work with light-hearted, fun, professional people.

TRY TO KEEP THE MEETING SHORT

It should be no longer than thirty minutes. I have had meetings drag on for two hours and that is just too long. Plus, it starts me thinking that this model could end up being a high maintenance situation. **Don't be shy about bringing a paper with your questions on it. Take notes because you will never remember everything that is said to you.** This is especially important when you are seeing several agencies in the same market. Things may start to jumble and crossover by the end of the day. Make sure to take notes immediately after leaving each agency.

At the end of the meeting, whether in person or over the phone, you will either have more steps that need to be taken in order to get signed or you will have a contract.

If they have additional requests of you, such as meeting with them in person, or your skin or shape needs work, or a photo shoot, let them know when and if you can do it. Then, give them an estimated time of when you will get back in contact with them.

CONTRACTS

PLEASE DO NOT SIGN A CONTRACT IMMEDIATELY.
NEVER DO THIS.

A contract is a very serious piece of paper. **It should always be read thoroughly and given consideration for a period of time.** If you are underage, make sure to read your contract thoroughly and have your parents go over anything you do not understand. Make sure to take time before signing the contract. **Even if you are absolutely sure this is exactly what you want, make sure you have the same response in twenty-four hours.** Sometimes just a day gives you a different perspective. The agency wants you to be just as sure as they are about representation.

Smaller markets tend to have pretty basic contracts. Some of the larger market contracts can be more complex because larger money bookings are involved. **A contract is an agreement for a specific amount of time to safeguard both you and the agency, and a contract should read that way.** It is ensuring you and the agency of both of your responsibilities -- whether things go right or wrong. The contract should spell out responsibilities, monies and commission percentages, payment procedures, penalties and the legal obligations of both parties.

KEY THINGS TO LOOK FOR:

+ **The length of the contract.** Please remember nothing is in stone. If you are not comfortable with the length of a contract, you may be able to get it changed. Most healthy contracts are for a one or two-year period. I personally believe anything longer is too long. **I think that two years is fair, especially when developing a new talent.** By the two-year mark, you both should know if it is working or not.

+ **How to break the contract.** This is key because most contracts automatically reinstate annually if you don't give notice otherwise. **Most agencies insist that you adhere to their policies in regards to cancellation.** For example, if it says you must give forty-five days written notice that you are leaving when the contract expires, then that is what you have to do. Know this information well.

Unfortunately it is not the same from the agency's side. They can let you go at any point of time. Most contracts will state specifically the reasons you could be cancelled — unprofessionalism, unavailability, not confirming enough jobs, bad work performance, not making enough money, etc.

Usually you can break a contract for similar reasons but you still need to follow proper procedure. For instance, if you feel the agency is being unprofessional, you would want to send a certified letter stating this and the amount of time you are giving for it to be rectified or you will seek other representation .

+ **Monies** – how they are procured from the client, how the monies are broken down to your paycheck and the agency's commission percentage, and how you are paid. **A typical example is that most models in the U.S.A. are paid 80% of their paycheck with the agency earning**

20% commission. In primary markets, most models are paid weekly but they are not paid for extra usage fees until the client pays. Usage fees are for additional fees other than the booking itself. One example of a usage fee would be doing a day booking for a catalogue at one set rate and the client decides to use one of the shots for an additional advertisement in magazines. That extra usage for the magazine ad would be an extra fee.

✦ **One special note about your monies:** Agencies are not an employment agency. **You, in essence, employ the agency and you are responsible for your own taxes.** Make sure to hire a good entertainment-oriented accountant so that you get all the breaks that go along with our business as well as being your own company.

✦ **Your responsibilities.** Know this well and make sure you can follow through on all of those stated. Once you sign your name, you are responsible to adhere to each and every one of them.

✦ **Your exclusive representation.** This means that you can only be represented in the markets stated in the contract by that agency. **Most contracts state exclusivity for only the city where the agency is based.** Sometimes contracts state a larger area. For example, your Los Angeles agency may state they represent you exclusively for the entire West Coast. You will need to discuss this before signing if you want the option for other agency representation in other West Coast cities. Perhaps consider giving the agency a timeline to prove they can procure work in the other markets named in the contract.

✦ **Mother agency.** Most contracts include this. **This means they are responsible for career management and placement in all markets.** If you don't want an agency to be your mother agent, you will have to discuss this with the agency before signing and have that part taken out. I believe that the first agency you sign with should be your mother agency, especially if they are doing all of the footwork. Otherwise, you should pursue other agencies or markets until you find the right mother agency for you.

You always have the option to have your contract read over by an attorney. I recommend my models have their New York contracts read over by an attorney because it is the most lucrative advertising and campaign market in the world. With other markets, I insist that a model learns to read his or her contract. Contracts from international markets are difficult to understand. **Make sure you understand what you are signing. KNOW YOUR BUSINESS. YOU ARE IN CHARGE OF YOUR OWN COMPANY!**

Read over the contract, and if you don't understand certain legal terms or a certain part of the contract, call the agency and have it explained. If you feel it doesn't read like the agency says, tell them you are putting an asterisk on that part of the contract, crossing out what you don't understand and stating it in a simpler, understandable translation than you were just reading, and initial it. This will safeguard you from being told something that you do not see or understand in the writing.

I feel two weeks is as long as a contract should take to look over. If you have many options as far as agencies that want you, this process could drag out a little longer.

If you are confused about which agency to choose, I always recommend writing down two questions that you can ask each agency. Then, make notes on their answers and this should help you with the elimination process. If you feel confused, you will just have to learn to trust your own instincts. Usually, you have a sense of where you belong. You just get confused along the way.

When **In Demand**

Ithink the hardest thing for potential models with lots of agencies pursuing them is the decision making process of picking the one agency that will start their career and be their mother agency.

The entire process of agencies trying to acquire you for representation can become a circus. You will have to try to separate yourself from the entire hullabaloo that goes on trying to get you signed to an agency. It can get very cheerleader-esque and rah rah. **At some point, getting down to business will have to kick in,** and later, the reality that you are one of thousands of amazing models in the world trying to make it in fashion will slam you in the face.

It is best for you to look at these agencies from perhaps the lowest possible results. In other words, if you don't make it to supermodel level, how will this agency represent you? What if you decide to get married and move to a smaller market, how will this agency handle you? If you aren't making the mark everyone thought you would, how will this agency help you fight to get there?

I have been blessed with being mother agent to models with amazing potential. Some have made it to the top and a lot have not. When models so many agencies after them, then they choose, then the "we want you, future supermodel!" circus stops, they are usually disappointed because they thought they were going to be this glamorous, overnight sensation. They thought the agency would bother them daily and bookings would immediately surface. It cannot be. Beginning steps in a new career do not work that way.

Think of it like being the star quarterback from your high school team. Colleges go after you tooth and nail. They tell you they see you as a future pro-bowler. You pick the college you want. As a freshman, do you start as the quarterback? Probably not. It usually takes two to three years for you to achieve this position. Do they stroke your ego while you are low man on the totem pole for three years? Most likely not. So, why does the high school quarterback understand this and not the brand new model with so much potential? More importantly, why do the parents not understand this? At some point, it boils down to straight business. **No matter how much potential you have, no matter how hard agencies fight to get you, it will take YOU to achieve the great results with hard work, perseverance and patience.** Be aware of this and make sure to make rational, level-headed, solidly based decisions for yourself and your career.

Misconceptions **About the Business**

I want to leave you with a few misconceptions that drive me crazy once a young hopeful starts in our business.

THIS BUSINESS HAPPENS FAST AND SHOULD COST ME NOTHING.

Be prepared to balance career ambition with patience and do not ignore the wisdom of investing in your future. **Why is it with our business that I continually hear models or parents say after only one year and maybe an investment of $2,000 that returns seem too low and they're quitting the business?** It blows my mind. Often college is considered by parents to be more of a "sure thing". I think to myself, "It is?" Although agents are all pro-school, what exactly is so sure about college? I went to top universities in the U.S.A. and Paris and my parents spent somewhere over $100,000 on my education (now, that is an investment!). After four years of college, my first job offer in New York City was for under $13,000 a year. Yes, I have a very successful career now but it took years to get there. **This business, like all others, takes time and investment -- don't expect a cash windfall the first few months or the first few years.**

IN THREE MONTHS, I WILL KNOW IF I AM GOING TO MAKE IT IN THE BUSINESS.

Okay, you go to college and you want to be a chemist. You are in your first semester of Chemistry I and the course takes twelve weeks. You ace all of your exams. Does that mean you are going to be a top chemist? Now, let's look at the opposite scenario: You are failing miserably, not understanding the work at all, and do not do well on your first exams. Does that mean you are not going to make it? Of course, it can give you an inkling of an idea either way but if you want to make it, you can. You just have to either keep up the good work or work harder. The results will not happen in three months.

The same holds true for the modeling industry. Think of it as going to school. Freshman year you are getting a grip, figuring things out, learning how to process information to aim for the success you want, and sometimes reorganizing yourself to make things work better. Sophomore year you are refining your skills, narrowing in a bit more to what you are good at, and hopefully starting to see yourself inch towards the 50-yard line. Junior year should be going pretty well where you are seeing some good marks telling you that you are on the right path. Senior year should be the culmination of the final touches of all of your hard work to the success you want to achieve.

Give it a good four years if you really have what it takes and keep your ambitions high.

AM BEAUTIFUL, AND THAT'S ALL IT TAKES.

I don't care if you are the best looking guy in your class, you were voted homecoming king, every girl in your high school wants to date you, and you're going to be valedictorian. That doesn't mean if you put little effort into this business, you are going to make it. Did you put little effort into becoming the best student in your class? **Think of all the cities and all the countries in the world with good looking people. Think of how many of them want to become a successful model.** Just take the state you live in and multiply all the schools and all the counties and all the cities, and think of how competitive it is in your state alone. If you are trying to become "the Tom Cruise of acting" in modeling, you can expect a lot of rejection, being pushed down, having to get up, wiping the dust off of yourself, and trying to climb up the stairs again and again. **It takes strong conviction to make it in a business that so many people want into, and especially where the competition is so intense.**

WORK ALL THE TIME IN MY SMALL MARKET. IT WILL BE THE SAME FOR ME IN ANY LARGER MARKET.

Usually, not true at all. Smaller markets don't have as much high level competition and clients have to choose from models who don't always have editorial portfolios, or models who are not as sophisticated as larger markets. **I will see a model that works all the time in Kansas City go to New York City and get turned down by every agency.** You have to research each and every market to see if you are a fit.

WORK ALL THE TIME IN MY BIG MARKET. IT WILL BE THE SAME FOR ME IN ANY SMALLER MARKET.

This one is not always true either. Many times, models that are international, editorial and geared towards larger, more sophisticated markets may end up being too much for a smaller market. Smaller markets tend to want models that are more relatable and more commercial lifestyle than elegant, refined and edgy models of primary markets.

LOOKS MATTER AND WHO I AM DOESN'T.

Wrong, wrong, wrong. Agencies and clients want to work with nice, professional, good personality people. Keep this in mind: Do you want to go on a trip with someone who is mean or snotty for one day? How about seven days? **A client doesn't care what you look like or where you have modeled if you can't be nice at a booking.** Learning to be professional, nice, and smart enough not to burn bridges is the best way to work in our business.

IF I GET BOOKED ONCE WITH A BIG CLIENT, I AM ON MY WAY TO BEING SUCCESSFUL.

Yes, having a client give you that first break is essential but it's not the key to success. **Repeat bookings are the formula for success.** I have seen models who book one time with many top clients never be rebooked. These models end up out of the business quite quickly if they don't figure out what it is that is stopping them from being rebooked. Usually it is either being too stiff and not moving well or being unprofessional. Being unprofessional can include a number of things, but mainly it boils down to just not being nice.

MY TIME IS MORE IMPORTANT THAN EVERYONE ELSE'S.

If you have this attitude, you will surely end up out of our business quicker than anything. Agents work their butts off and are overall pretty selfless creatures, almost bonafide personal secretaries except that they are secretaries for a number of people and not just one. Clients have rigorous schedules that need to be adhered to. If you think being late, not calling back, not showing up, bossing people around or in any other way just being downright selfish and rude is going to help your career, please think again.

MY AGENCY SHOULD KNOW WHAT I WANT.

Agents are not mind readers. If you are unhappy about something or want something specifically, tell your agency. Communication is essential from both sides to optimize your career's success.

MY AGENCY WILL ADVANCE EVERYTHING FOR ME.

Why do some new young hopefuls, even after reading this book, assume that everyone is waiting for them and will pay for everything? I have said this so many times,and will say it again: The competition is fierce -- from beginning to end. If you take the attitude that you're not interested unless they advance to pay your entire way or give it to you for free, you are most likely never going to get very far in the business. Invest in yourself and your career. It is no different than going to college. There are scholarships out there. Just make sure you are exactly what they want and be prepared to work hard.

: C h a p t e r 13 :
Final **Thoughts**

This is the hardest part of the book. Have I told you enough? Will this book help you get where you want to go? What have I forgotten?

I love this business. It is always changing. There is no set route. Challenges are an everyday event. It is up one moment and then down another. I always wanted to be a part of an industry that constantly challenges me to be the best I can be, that forces me to grow continually, that asks me to learn from my peers and the generations after me, and that is exciting, interesting and unusual.

I challenge you to be the best you can be. There hasn't been a new American supermodel in over a decade. You will have to want it badly, focus hard, create your craft strong, be an absolute professional and have very high ambitions in order to win out against the fierce competition from top international countries.

Lastly, you will learn most of this business by doing and experiencing it firsthand. You will have to be what they want and at the same time, you will have to be able to express who you innately are. You get out of this world what you put into it. If you have a negative attitude, that is what you will get back. In the long run, sending out a positive message in a loving way always wins. Good luck and God bless. Thank you.

- Marcia Rothschild Moellers / interscout@aol.com

Marcia **Rothschild Moellers** has been an agent for over two decades. Marcia grew up in Crete, Illinois, and attended college at DePauw University in Indiana and The Sorbonne in Paris. She has worked in New York City, Chicago, Atlanta, Denver, and Arizona. She has been employed by top agencies, such as Ford, IMG and Elite. She currently works for Donna Baldwin Talent in Denver and Bravo Models in Tokyo. She and her husband, James, split their time between their beloved Rocky Mountain National Park in Colorado and their farm in Ossian, Iowa. They have three wonderful children, Jake, Morgane and Madison.

MODEL CREDITS

A BIG THANK YOU TO MODELS FROM INTERSCOUT AND DONNA BALDWIN TALENT

2237 W. 30th Ave. Denver, Colorado 80211
(303) 561-1199 www.donnabaldwin.com

Brandy
Armstrong

Elvis Edwards

Lauren
Herasimtschuk

Abby McCary

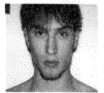

Cassidy
Klements

Heather Knapp

Kacie
Lancaster

Caley &
Courtney Fisher

Neil Marks

Jamie McClung

Ian McNeil

TJ Harvey

Claire Ryan

Rani Sanderson

Madison Garton

Riann Cousino

Alex Browne

Jenna Reeves

Allison Zebelian